Lectionary
Advent 2024 to the eve of Advent 2025 (Year C)

Church House Publishing

Published by	Church House Publishing Church House Great Smith Street London SW1P 3AZ
Compilation ©	*The Archbishops' Council 2024*
ISBN	978-0-7151-2418-5 Standard 978-0-7151-2419-2 Large 978-0-7151-2420-8 E-ISBN

Authorization	The Common Worship Calendar and Lectionaries are authorized pursuant to Canon B 2 of the Canons of the Church of England for use until further resolution of the General Synod of the Church of England.
Copyright and Acknowledgements	The Revised Common Lectionary is copyright © The Consultation on Common Texts: 1992. The Church of England adaptations to the Principal Service Lectionary are copyright © The Archbishops' Council, as are the Second and Third Service Lectionaries, the Weekday Lectionary for Morning and Evening Prayer and the Additional Weekday Lectionary. The Daily Eucharistic Lectionary derives, with some adaptation, from the Ordo Lectionum Missae of the Roman Catholic Church and is reproduced by permission of The International Commission on English in the Liturgy. Edited by Peter Moger Designed by Derek Birdsall & John Morgan/Omnific Typeset by RefineCatch Ltd, Bungay, Suffolk Printed in England by Core Publications Ltd

Contents of this booklet

This booklet gives details of the full range of possibilities envisaged in the liturgical calendar and lectionary of Common Worship. Its use as a tool for the preparation of worship will require the making of several choices based first on the general celebration of the Christian year by the Church of England as a whole; second on the customary pattern of calendar in the diocese, parish and place of worship; and third on the pattern of services locally.

The **first column** comprises the Calendar of the Church with the days of the year. Observances that are mandatory are printed either in **bold** type (Sundays), in **bold** type (Principal Feasts and Holy Days) or in roman (Festivals). Optional celebrations (Lesser Festivals) and Commemorations are printed in ordinary roman type and *italic* type respectively.

The **second column** comprises (a) the readings and psalms for the Principal Service on Sundays, Principal Feasts and Holy Days, and Festivals, and (b) Holy Communion readings and psalms for other days of the week. On the Sundays after Trinity, the Old Testament reading and its psalm are divided into two smaller columns, indicating a choice between a 'continuous' reading week by week or a reading 'related' to the Gospel for that day.

The **third column** comprises (a) the Third Service readings and psalms for Sundays, Principal Feasts and Holy Days, and Festivals, and (b) the readings and psalms for weekday Morning Prayer.

The **fourth column** comprises (a) the Second Service readings and psalms for Sundays, Principal Feasts and Holy Days, and Festivals, and (b) the readings and psalms for weekday Evening Prayer.

An **Additional Weekday Lectionary**, intended particularly for use in places of worship that attract occasional rather than daily worshippers, is provided on pages 70–77. It may be used either at Morning or Evening Prayer.

Common of the Saints

General readings and psalms for saints' days can be found on pages 79–83; for some particular celebrations, other readings are suggested there.

Special Occasions

Readings and psalms for special occasions can be found on pages 84–85.

Liturgical colours

Appropriate liturgical colours are suggested in this booklet. They are not mandatory; traditional or local use may be followed.

Colours are indicated by single letters: the first (always upper case) for the season or Festival; and occasionally a second (lower case) for an optional celebration on that day. Thus, for example, *Gr* for the celebration of a Lesser Festival whose liturgical colour is red, in an otherwise 'green' season.

The following abbreviations are used:

G	Green
P or p	Purple or Violet
P(La)	Purple or Lent array
R or r	Red
W or w	White (Gold is indicated where its use would be appropriate)

Notes on the Lectionary

Sundays, Principal Feasts and Holy Days and Festivals

Three sets of psalms and readings are provided for each Sunday, Principal Feast or Holy Day and Festival.

The **Principal Service lectionary** (based on the Revised Common Lectionary) is intended for use at the principal service of the day (whether this service is Holy Communion or some other authorized form). In most Church communities, this is likely to be the mid-morning service, but the minister is free to decide which service time normally constitutes the Principal Service of the day. This lectionary may be used twice if required – for example, at an early celebration of Holy Communion and then again at a later one.

If only **two readings** are used at the Principal Service and that service is Holy Communion, the second reading must always be the Gospel reading. When the Principal Service lectionary is used at a service other than Holy Communion, the Gospel reading need not always be chosen.

The **Second Service lectionary** is intended for a second main service. In many churches, this lectionary may be the appropriate provision for a Sunday afternoon or evening service. A Gospel reading is always provided so that this lectionary can, if necessary, be used where the second main service is a celebration of Holy Communion.

The **Third Service lectionary**, with shorter readings, is intended where a third set of psalms and readings is needed and is most appropriate for use at an office. A Gospel reading is not always provided, so this lectionary is not suitable for use at Holy Communion.

Weekdays

The Common Worship Weekday Lectionary authorized by the General Synod in 2005 comprises a lectionary (with psalms) for Holy Communion, a lectionary for Morning and Evening Prayer, and tables of psalms for Morning and Evening Prayer.

The **Daily Eucharistic Lectionary** (based on the Roman Catholic daily eucharistic lectionary) is a semi-continuous two-year lectionary with a wide use of scripture, though not complete coverage of the Bible. Two readings are provided for each day, the first from either the Old or New Testament, the second always a Gospel. Psalm provision is intended to be a brief response to the first reading. It is for use at Holy Communion normally in places with a daily or near-daily celebration with a regular congregation. It may also be used as an office lectionary.

The **lectionary for Morning and Evening Prayer** always provides two readings for each office, the first from the Old Testament and the second from the New Testament. These are generally in sequence. One of the New Testament readings for any particular day is from the Gospels.

The **psalms for Morning and Evening Prayer** follow a sequential pattern in Ordinary Time (apart from the period from All Saints to the beginning of Advent).

In the periods from All Saints until 18 December, from the Epiphany until the Presentation of Christ in the Temple (Candlemas), from Ash Wednesday until Palm Sunday, and from the Monday after Easter Week until Pentecost, there is a choice of psalms at Morning and Evening Prayer. The psalms printed first reflect the theme of the season. Alternatively, the psalms from the Ordinary Time cycle may be used. The two sets are separated by '*or*'.

From 19 December until the Epiphany and from the Monday of Holy Week until the Saturday of Easter Week, only seasonal psalms are provided.

Where more than one psalm is given, one psalm (printed in **bold**) may be used as the sole psalm at that office.

Guidance on how these options for saying the psalms are expressed typographically can be found in the 'Notes on the Lectionary' below.

A further cycle is provided (see table on page 86), which is largely the monthly sequential cycle of psalms given in the *Book of Common Prayer*.

A single psalm for use by those who only say one office each day is provided in Prayer During the Day in *Common Worship: Daily Prayer*.

An **Additional Weekday Lectionary**, intended particularly for use in places of worship that attract occasional rather than daily worshippers, is provided on pages 70–77. It can be used either at Morning or Evening Prayer. Psalmody is not provided and should be taken from provision outlined above.

Using the Lectionary tables

All **Bible references** (except to the Psalms) are to the *New Revised Standard Version* (New York, 1989). Those who use other Bible translations should check the verse numbers against the *NRSV*. Each reference gives book, chapter and verse, in that order.

References to the Psalms are to the Common Worship psalter, published in *Common Worship: Services and Prayers for the Church of England* (2000) and *Common Worship: Daily Prayer* (2005). A table showing the verse number differences between this and the psalter in the *Book of Common Prayer* is provided on the Common Worship website (https://www.churchofengland.org/prayer-and-worship/worship-texts-and-resources/common-worship/daily-prayer/psalter/psalter-verse).

Options in the provision of readings or psalms are presented in the following ways:

¶ square brackets [xx] give either optional additional verses or Psalms, or a shorter alternative;

¶ 'or' indicates a simple choice between two alternative readings or courses of psalms;

¶ a psalm printed in **bold** may be used as the sole psalm at that office;

¶ on weekdays a psalm printed in parentheses (xx) is omitted if it has been used as the opening canticle at that office;

¶ a psalm marked with an asterisk may be shortened if desired.

Where a reading from the **Apocrypha** is offered, an alternative Old Testament reading is provided.

In the choice of **readings other than the Gospel** reading, the minister should ensure that, in any year, a balance is maintained between readings from the Old and New Testaments and that, where a particular biblical book is appointed to be read over several weeks, the choice ensures that the continuity of one book is not lost.

On the Sundays after Trinity, the Principal Service Lectionary provides **alternative Old Testament readings and psalms.** References in the left-hand column (under the heading 'Continuous') offer a *semi-continuous* reading of Old Testament texts. Such a reading and its complementary psalmody stand independently of the other readings. References in the right-hand column (under the heading 'Related') *relate* the Old Testament reading and the psalm to the Gospel reading. One column should be followed for the whole sequence of Sundays after Trinity.

The Lectionary 2024–2025

The Sunday and festal readings for 1 December 2024 (the First Sunday of Advent) to 29 November 2025 (the eve of Advent Sunday) are from **Year C**, which offers a semi-continuous reading of Luke's Gospel at the Principal Service on Sundays throughout the year.

The weekday readings for Holy Communion are from **Year One** of the Daily Eucharistic Lectionary (DEL).

Office readings are from Table 2 of the Weekday Lectionary: at Morning Prayer, Old Testament 2b in Ordinary Time and 2a in Seasonal Time and New Testament 2; and, at Evening Prayer, Old Testament 1 and New Testament 1.

Notes on the Calendar 1 December 2024— 29 November 2025

These notes are based on the Rules to Order the Christian Year (*Common Worship: Times and Seasons*, pages 24–30).

Sundays

All Sundays celebrate the paschal mystery of the death and resurrection of the Lord. They also reflect the character of the seasons in which they are set.

Principal Feasts

On these days (printed in **bold**) Holy Communion is celebrated in every cathedral and at least one church in each benefice or, where benefices are held in plurality, in at least one church in at least one of those benefices, and this celebration, required by Canon B 14, may not be displaced by any other celebration, and may only be dispensed with in accordance with the provision of Canon B 14A.

Except in the case of Christmas Day and Easter Day, the celebration of the Feast *begins with Evening Prayer on the day before the Feast*, and the Collect at that Evening Prayer is that of the Feast. In the case of Christmas Eve and Easter Eve, there is proper liturgical provision (including a Collect) for the whole day.

The Epiphany may, for pastoral reasons, be celebrated on Sunday 5 January. **All Saints' Day** may be celebrated on Sunday 2 November (replacing the Fourth Sunday before Advent), with or without a supplementary celebration on Saturday 1 November.

Other Principal Holy Days

These days (printed in **bold**), and the liturgical provision for them, may not be displaced by any other celebration.

Ash Wednesday (5 March) and **Maundy Thursday** (17 April) are Principal Holy Days. On both these days Holy Communion is celebrated in every cathedral or parish church, except where there is dispensation under Canon B 14A.

Good Friday (18 April) is a Principal Holy Day.

Eastertide

The paschal character of **the Great Fifty Days of Easter**, from Easter Day (20 April) to Pentecost (8 June), should be celebrated throughout the season, and should not be displaced by other celebrations. No Festival day may be celebrated in Easter Week; and nor may any Festival – except for a Patronal or Dedication Festival – displace the celebration of a Sunday (a memorial of the resurrection) during Eastertide. The paschal character of the season should be retained on those weekdays when saints' days are celebrated.

The three days before Ascension Day (26–28 May) are customarily observed as **Rogation Days**, when prayer is offered for God's blessing on the fruits of the earth and on human labour.

The nine days **after Ascension Day until the eve of Pentecost** (30 May – 7 June) are observed as days of prayer and preparation for the celebration of the outpouring of the Holy Spirit.

Ordinary Time

Ordinary Time comprises two periods in the year: first, the period from the day after the Presentation of Christ in the Temple until the day before Ash Wednesday, and second, that from the day after Pentecost until the day before the First Sunday of Advent.

During Ordinary Time, there is no seasonal emphasis, except that the period between All Saints' Day and the First Sunday of Advent is a time to celebrate and reflect upon the reign of Christ in earth and heaven.

Festivals

These days (printed in roman), and the liturgical provision for them, are not usually displaced. For each day there is full liturgical provision for a Principal, Second and Third Service, and an optional so-called First Evening Prayer on the evening before the Festival where this is required.

Festivals may *not* be celebrated on Sundays in Advent, Lent or Eastertide, the Baptism of Christ, Ascension Day, Trinity Sunday or Christ the King, or weekdays between Palm Sunday and the Second Sunday of Easter.

Otherwise, Festivals falling on a Sunday – namely in 2025 Peter and Paul (falling on the Second Sunday after Trinity), Bartholomew (falling on the Tenth Sunday after Trinity), Holy Cross Day (falling on the Thirteenth Sunday after Trinity), and Matthew (falling on the Fourteenth Sunday after Trinity) – may be kept on that Sunday or transferred to the Monday (or, at the discretion of the minister, to the next suitable weekday).

Certain Festivals (namely, Matthias the Apostle, the Visit of the BVM to Elizabeth, Thomas the Apostle, and the Blessed Virgin Mary) have customary alternative dates (see page 8).

The Thursday after Trinity Sunday (19 June) may be observed as the **Day of Thanksgiving for the Institution of Holy Communion** (sometimes known as *Corpus Christi*), and may be kept as a Festival.

Other Celebrations

Mothering Sunday falls on the Fourth Sunday of Lent (30 March). Alternative prayers and readings are provided for the Principal Service. **Bible Sunday** may be celebrated on 26 October, replacing the Last Sunday after Trinity, and appropriate prayers and readings are provided.

Local Celebrations

The celebration of **the patron saint or the title of a church** is kept either as a Festival or as a Principal Feast.

The **Dedication Festival** of a church is the anniversary of the date of its dedication or consecration. This is kept either as a Festival or as a Principal Feast. When kept as Principal Feasts, the Patronal and Dedication Festivals may be transferred to the nearest Sunday, unless that day is already a Principal Feast or one of the following days: the First Sunday of Advent, the Baptism of Christ, the First Sunday of Lent, the Fifth Sunday of Lent, or Palm Sunday. If the actual date is not known, the Dedication Festival may be celebrated on 5 October (replacing the Sixteenth Sunday after Trinity), or on 26 October (replacing the Last Sunday after Trinity), or on a suitable date chosen locally. Readings can be found on page 78.

Harvest Thanksgiving may be celebrated on any Sunday in autumn, replacing the provision for that day, provided it does not displace any Principal Feast or Festival.

Diocesan and other local provision may be made in **the calendar of the saints** to supplement the general calendar, in accordance with Canon B 6, paragraph 5.

Lesser Festivals

Lesser Festivals (printed in ordinary roman type, in black) are observed in a manner appropriate to a particular place. Each is provided with a Collect, which may supersede the Collect of the week. For certain Lesser Festivals a complete set of Eucharistic readings is provided, and for others appropriate readings may be selected from the Common of the Saints (see pages 79–83). These readings may, at the minister's discretion, supersede the Daily Eucharistic Lectionary (DEL). The weekday psalms and readings at Morning and Evening Prayer are not usually superseded by those for Lesser Festivals, but at the minister's discretion psalms and readings provided on these days for use at Holy Communion may be used instead at Morning or Evening Prayer.

The minister may be selective in the Lesser Festivals that are observed and may also keep some, or all of them, as Commemorations, perhaps especially in Advent, Lent and Easter where the character of the season ought to be sustained. If the Day of Thanksgiving for the Institution of Holy Communion (19 June) is not kept as a Festival, it may be kept as a Lesser Festival.

When a Lesser Festival falls on a Principal Feast or Holy Day, a Festival, a Sunday, or on a weekday between Palm Sunday and the Second Sunday of Easter, its celebration is normally omitted for that year. However, where there is sufficient reason, it may, at the discretion of the minister, be celebrated on the nearest available day.

Commemorations

Commemorations (printed in *italic*) are made by a mention in prayers of intercession. They are not provided with Collect, Psalm and Readings, and do not replace the usual weekday provision at Holy Communion or at Morning and Evening Prayer.

The minister may be selective in the Commemorations that are made.

Only where there is an established celebration in the wider Church or where the day has a special local significance may a Commemoration be observed as a Lesser Festival, with liturgical provision from the Common of the Saints (pages 79–83).

In designating a Commemoration as a Lesser Festival, the minister must remember the need to maintain the spirit of the season, especially of Advent, Lent and Easter.

Days of Discipline and Self-Denial

The weekdays of Lent and every Friday in the year are days of discipline and self-denial, with the exception of Principal Feasts, Festivals outside Lent, and Fridays from Easter Day to Pentecost. The day preceding a Principal Feast may also be appropriately kept as a day of discipline and self–denial in preparation for the Feast.

Ember Days

Ember Days should be kept, under the bishop's directions, in the week before an ordination as days of prayer for those to be ordained deacon or priest.

Ember Days may also be kept even when there is no ordination in the diocese as more general days of prayer for those who serve the Church in its various ministries, both ordained and lay, and for vocations. Traditionally they have been observed on the Wednesday, Friday and Saturday in the week before the Third Sunday of Advent, the Second Sunday of Lent, and the Sundays nearest to 29 June and 29 September.

Notes on Collects

For a table showing where the Collects and Post Communions are published, see page 78.

Where a Collect ends 'through Jesus Christ … now and for ever', the minister may omit the longer (trinitarian) ending and use the shorter ending, 'through Jesus Christ our Lord', to which the people respond, 'Amen'. The longer ending, however, is to be preferred at a service of Holy Communion.

The Collect for each Sunday is used at Evening Prayer on the Saturday preceding, except where that Saturday is a Principal Feast, or a Festival, or the eve of Christmas Day or Easter Day. The Collect for each Sunday is also used on the weekdays following, except where other provision is made.

Abbreviations used in this book

Alt	Alternative
BVM	Blessed Virgin Mary
DEL	Daily Eucharistic Lectionary
EP	Evening Prayer
G	Green
HC	Holy Communion: *used where additional references are given to provide alternative texts for use at a celebration of Holy Communion (most often the provision of a psalm or gospel)*
MP	Morning Prayer
P or p	Purple or Violet
P(La)	Purple or Lent Array
Ps & Pss	Psalmody
R or r	Red
W or w	White (Gold is indicated where its use would be appropriate)

Alternative dates

The following may be celebrated on the alternative dates indicated:

Thomas the Apostle
– on 21 December 2024 instead of 3 July 2025
Matthias the Apostle
– on 24 February instead of 14 May
The Visit of the Blessed Virgin Mary to Elizabeth
– on 2 July instead of 31 May
Cuthbert
– On 4 September instead of 20 March
The Blessed Virgin Mary
– on 8 September instead of 15 August

If any of the four festivals is celebrated on the alternative date these provisions should be used on the principal date:

Holy Communion	Morning Prayer	Evening Prayer
If Thomas the Apostle is celebrated on Saturday 21 December 2024 the following provision is used on Thursday 3 July 2025 (G):		
Genesis 22.1–9	Psalms 56, **57** (63*)	Psalms 61, **62**, 64
Psalm 116.1–7	Job 23	Judges 6.1–24
Matthew 9.1– 8	Romans 10.11–end	Luke 14.1–11
If Matthias the Apostle is celebrated on Tuesday 24 February the following provision is used on Wednesday 14 May (W):		
Acts 12.24—13.5	Psalm **135** *or* **119.57–80**	11 Psalms **47**, 48 *or* **59**, 60 (67)
Psalm 67	Deuteronomy 10.12–end	Exodus 33
John 12.44–end	Ephesians 5.1–14	Luke 3.15–22
If The Visit of the Blessed Virgin Mary to Elizabeth is celebrated on Wednesday 2 July the following provision is used on Saturday 31 May (W):		
Acts 18.22–end	Psalms 21, **47** *or* 96, **97**, 100	Psalms 84, **85** *or* **104**
Psalm 47.1–2, 7–end	Numbers 21.4–9	Deuteronomy 30
John 16.23–28	Luke 7.18–35	1 John 2.7–17
	** Numbers 11.16–17, 24–29; 1 Corinthians 2*	
If The Blessed Virgin Mary is celebrated on Monday 8 September the following provision is used on Friday 15 August (G):		
Joshua 24.1–13	Psalm **31**	Psalm **35**
Psalm 136.1–3	Ezekiel 34.17–end	1 Samuel 17.31–54
Matthew 19.3–12	James 4.13—5.6	Luke 24.13–35

Key to the Tables

For guidance on how the options for saying the psalms are expressed typographically, see page 5.

Sundays (and Principal Feasts, other Principal Holy Days, and Festivals)

Day	Date	*Colour*	Principal Service	3rd Service	2nd Service
Day	**Date** Sunday / **Feast** † / Festival ††	*Colour*	Main service of the day: Holy Communion, Morning Prayer, Evening Prayer, or a Service of the Word	Shorter Readings, an Office lectionary probably used at Morning Prayer where Holy Communion is the Principal Service	2nd main service, probably used at Evening Prayer; adaptable for Holy Communion

† Principal Feasts and other Principal Holy Days are printed in **bold**.
†† Festivals are printed in roman typeface.

Weekdays

Day	Date	*Colour*	Holy Communion	Morning Prayer	Evening Prayer
Day	**Date**	*Colour*	Weekday readings	Psalms and readings for Morning Prayer	Psalms and readings for Evening Prayer

Lesser Festival ‡* [optional]
Commemoration ‡‡ [optional]

‡ Lesser Festivals are printed in roman typeface, in black.
‡‡ Commemorations are printed in *italics*.
* The ascriptions given to holy men and women in the Calendar (such as martyr, teacher of the faith, etc.) have often been abbreviated in this booklet for reasons of space. The particular ascription given is there to be helpful if needing to choose Collects and readings from Common of the Saints; where several ascriptions are used (e.g. bishop and martyr), traditionally the last ascription given is the most important and therefore the guiding one. The full ascriptions may be found in the Calendar, which is printed in *Common Worship: Times and Seasons* (pages 7–22), *Common Worship: Festivals* (pages 5–20) and *Common Worship: Daily Prayer* (pages 5–16). These incorporate minor corrections made since the publication of the Calendar in *Common Worship: Services and Prayers for the Church of England* (pages 5–16).

Advent 1

			Principal Service	3rd Service	2nd Service
Sunday	**1 December** **1st Sunday of Advent**	*P*	Jeremiah 33.14–16 Psalm 25.1–9 1 Thessalonians 3.9–end Luke 21.25–36	Psalm 44 Isaiah 51.4–11 Romans 13.11–end	Psalm 9 [*or* 9.1–8] Joel 3.9–end Revelation 14.13—15.4 *HC* John 3.1–17
			Holy Communion	**Morning Prayer**	**Evening Prayer**
Monday	**2 December**	*P*	Isaiah 2.1–5 Psalm 122 Matthew 8.5–11	Psalms **50**, 54 *or* **1**, 2, 3 Isaiah 42.18–end Revelation 19	Psalms 70, **71** *or* **4**, 7 Isaiah 25.1–9 Matthew 12.1–21
Tuesday	**3 December** *Francis Xavier, missionary, 1552*	*P*	Isaiah 11.1–10 Psalm 72.1–4, 18–19 Luke 10.21–24	Psalms **80**, 82 *or* **5**, 6 (8) Isaiah 43.1–13 Revelation 20	Psalms **74**, 75 *or* **9**, 10* Isaiah 26.1–13 Matthew 12.22–37
Wednesday	**4 December** *John of Damascus, monk, teacher of the faith, c.749* *Nicholas Ferrar, deacon, founder of the Little Gidding Community, 1637*	*P*	Isaiah 25.6–10*a* Psalm 23 Matthew 15.29–37	Psalms 5, **7** *or* **119.1–32** Isaiah 43.14–end Revelation 21.1–8	Psalms 76, **77** *or* **11**, 12, 13 Isaiah 28.1–13 Matthew 12.38–end
Thursday	**5 December**	*P*	Isaiah 26.1–6 Psalm 118.18–27*a* Matthew 7.21, 24–27	Psalms **42**, 43 *or* 14, **15**, 16 Isaiah 44.1–8 Revelation 21.9–21	Psalms **40**, 46 *or* **18*** Isaiah 28.14–end Matthew 13.1–23
Friday	**6 December** Nicholas, bishop, c.326 (see p.81)	*Pw*	Isaiah 29.17–end Psalm 27.1–4, 16–17 Matthew 9.27–31	Psalms **25**, 26 *or* 17, **19** Isaiah 44.9–23 Revelation 21.22—22.5	Psalms 16, **17** *or* **22** Isaiah 29.1–14 Matthew 13.24–43
Saturday	**7 December** Ambrose, bishop, teacher of the faith, 397 (see p.80)	*Pw*	Isaiah 30.19–21, 23–26 Psalm 146.4–9 Matthew 9.35—10.1, 6–8	Psalms **9** (10) *or* 20, 21, **23** Isaiah 44.24—45.13 Revelation 22.6–end	Psalms **27**, 28 *or* **24**, 25 Isaiah 29.15–end Matthew 13.44–end

Day	Date	Colour	Principal Service	3rd Service	2nd Service
Sunday	**8 December** **2nd Sunday of Advent**	*P*	Baruch 5 *or* Malachi 3.1–4 *Canticle*: Benedictus Philippians 1.3–11 Luke 3.1–6	Psalm 80 Isaiah 64.1–7 Matthew 11.2–11	Psalms 75 [76] Isaiah 40.1–11 Luke 1.1–25
			Holy Communion	**Morning Prayer**	**Evening Prayer**
Monday	**9 December**	*P*	Isaiah 35 Psalm 85.7–end Luke 5.17–26	Psalm **44** *or* 27, **30** Isaiah 45.14–end 1 Thessalonians 1	Psalms **144**, 146 *or* 26, **28**, 29 Isaiah 30.1–18 Matthew 14.1–12
Tuesday	**10 December**	*P*	Isaiah 40.1–11 Psalm 96.1, 10–end Matthew 18.12–14	Psalms **56**, 57 *or* 32, **36** Isaiah 46 1 Thessalonians 2.1–12	Psalms **11**, 12, 13 *or* **33** Isaiah 30.19–end Matthew 14.13–end
Wednesday	**11 December** Ember Day	*P*	Isaiah 40.25–end Psalm 103.8–13 Matthew 11.28–end	Psalms **62**, 63 *or* **34** Isaiah 47 1 Thessalonians 2.13–end	Psalms **10**, 14 *or* **119.33–56** Isaiah 31 Matthew 15.1–20
Thursday	**12 December**	*P*	Isaiah 41.13–20 Psalm 145.1, 8–13 Matthew 11.11–15	Psalms 53, **54**, 60 *or* **37*** Isaiah 48.1–11 1 Thessalonians 3	Psalm **73** *or* 39, **40** Isaiah 32 Matthew 15.21–28
Friday	**13 December** Lucy, martyr, 304 (see p.79) *Samuel Johnson, moralist, 1784* Ember Day	*Pr*	Isaiah 48.17–19 Psalm 1 Matthew 11.16–19	Psalms 85, **86** *or* **31** Isaiah 48.12–end 1 Thessalonians 4.1–12	Psalms 82, **90** *or* **35** Isaiah 33.1–22 Matthew 15.29–end
Saturday	**14 December** John of the Cross, poet, teacher of the faith, 1591 (see p.80) Ember Day	*Pw*	Ecclesiasticus 48.1–4, 9–11 *or* 2 Kings 2.9–12 Psalm 80.1–4, 18–19 Matthew 17.10–13	Psalm **145** *or* 41, **42**, 43 Isaiah 49.1–13 1 Thessalonians 4.13–end	Psalms 93, **94** *or* 45, **46** Isaiah 35 Matthew 16.1–12

Advent 3

			Principal Service	3rd Service	2nd Service
Sunday	**15 December** **3rd Sunday of Advent**	*P*	Zephaniah 3.14–end *Canticle*: Isaiah 12.2–end [*or* Psalm 146.4–end] Philippians 4.4–7 Luke 3.7–18	Psalms 12, 14 Isaiah 25.1–9 1 Corinthians 4.1–5	Psalms 50.1–6 [62] Isaiah 35 Luke 1.57–66 [67–end]
			Holy Communion	**Morning Prayer**	**Evening Prayer**
Monday	**16 December**	*P*	Numbers 24.2–7, 15–17 Psalm 25.3–8 Matthew 21.23–27	Psalm **40** *or* **44** Isaiah 49.14–25 1 Thessalonians 5.1–11	Psalms 25, **26** *or* **47**, 49 Isaiah 38. 1–8, 21–22 Matthew 16.13–end
Tuesday	**17 December** *O Sapientia* *Eglantyne Jebb, social reformer, founder of 'Save The Children', 1928*	*P*	Genesis 49.2, 8–10 Psalm 72.1–5, 18–19 Matthew 1.1–17	Psalms **70**, 74 *or* **48**, 52 Isaiah 50 1 Thessalonians 5.12–end	Psalms **50**, 54 *or* **50** Isaiah 38. 9–20 Matthew 17.1–13
Wednesday	**18 December** *O Adonai*	*P*	Jeremiah 23.5–8 Psalm 72. 1–2, 12–13, 18–end Matthew 1.18–24	Psalms **75**, 96 *or* **119.57–80** Isaiah 51.1–8 2 Thessalonians 1	Psalms 25, **82** *or* **59**, 60 (67) Isaiah 39 Matthew 17.14–21
				From Thursday 19 December until the Epiphany the seasonal psalmody must be used at Morning and Evening Prayer.	
Thursday	**19 December** *O Radix Jesse*	*P*	Judges 13.2–7, 24–end Psalm 71.3–8 Luke 1.5–25	Psalms 144, **146** Isaiah 51.9–16 2 Thessalonians 2	Psalms 10, **57** Zephaniah 1.1—2.3 Matthew 17.22–end
Friday	**20 December** *O Clavis David*	*P*	Isaiah 7.10–14 Psalm 24.1–6 Luke 1.26–38	Psalms **46**, 95 Isaiah 51.17–end 2 Thessalonians 3	Psalms **4**, 9 Zephaniah 3.1–13 Matthew 18.1–20
Saturday	**21 December** *O Oriens*	*P*	Zephaniah 3.14–18 Psalm 33.1–4, 11–12, 20–end Luke 1.39–45	Psalms **121**, 122, 123 Isaiah 52.1–12 Jude	Psalms 80, **84** Zephaniah 3.14–end Matthew 18.21–end

Day	Date	Colour	Principal Service	3rd Service	2nd Service
Sunday	**22 December** **4th Sunday of Advent** *O Rex Gentium*	*P*	Micah 5.2–5*a* *Canticle*: Magnificat *or* Psalm 80.1–8 Hebrews 10.5–10 Luke 1.39–45 [46–55]	Psalm 144 Isaiah 32.1–8 Revelation 22.6–end	Psalms 123 [131] Isaiah 10.33—11.10 Matthew 1.18–end
			Holy Communion	**Morning Prayer**	**Evening Prayer**
Monday	**23 December** *O Emmanuel*	*P*	Malachi 3.1–4; 4.5–end Psalm 25.3–9 Luke 1.57–66	Psalms 128, 129, **130**, 131 Isaiah 52.13—end of 53 2 Peter 1.1–15	Psalm **89.1–37** Malachi 1.1, 6–end Matthew 19.1–12
Tuesday	**24 December** **Christmas Eve**	*P*	*Morning Eucharist only:* 2 Samuel 7.1–5, 8–11, 16 Psalm 89.2, 19–27 Acts 13.16–26 Luke 1.67–79	Psalms **45**, 113 Isaiah 54 2 Peter 1.16—2.3	Psalm **85** Zechariah 2 Revelation 1.1–8
			Principal Service	**3rd Service**	**2nd Service**
Wednesday	**25 December** **Christmas Day**	*Gold or W*	*Any of the following three sets of Principal Service readings may be used on the evening of Christmas Eve and on Christmas Day. Set III should be used at some point during the celebration.* **Set I**: Isaiah 9.2–7; Psalm 96; Titus 2.11–14; Luke 2.1–14 [15–20] **Set II**: Isaiah 62.6–end; Psalm 97; Titus 3.4–7; Luke 2. [1–7] 8–20 **Set III**: Isaiah 52.7–10; Psalm 98; Hebrews 1.1–4 [5–12]; John 1.1–14	*MP* Psalms **110**, 117 Isaiah 62.1–5 Matthew 1.18–end	*EP* Psalm 8 Isaiah 65.17–25 Philippians 2.5–11 *or* Luke 2.1–20 *if it has not been used at the principal service of the day*
Thursday	**26 December** Stephen, deacon, first martyr	*R*	2 Chronicles 24.20–22 *or* Acts 7.51–end Psalm 119.161–168 Acts 7.51–end *or* Galatians 2.16*b*–20 Matthew 10.17–22	*MP* Psalms **13**, 31.1–8, 150 Jeremiah 26.12–15 Acts 6	*EP* Psalms 57, **86** Genesis 4.1–10 Matthew 23.34–end
Friday	**27 December** John, Apostle and Evangelist	*W*	Exodus 33.7–11*a* Psalm 117 1 John 1 John 21.19*b*–end	*MP* Psalms **21**, 147.13–end Exodus 33.12–end 1 John 2.1–11	*EP* Psalm **97** Isaiah 6.1–8 1 John 5.1–12
Saturday	**28 December** The Holy Innocents	*R*	Jeremiah 31.15–17 Psalm 124 1 Corinthians 1.26–29 Matthew 2.13–18	*MP* Psalms **36**, 146 Baruch 4.21–27 *or* Genesis 37.13–20 Matthew 18.1–10	*EP* Psalms 123, **128** Isaiah 49.14–25 Mark 10.13–16

Christmas 1

		Principal Service	3rd Service	2nd Service
Sunday	**29 December** W **1st Sunday of Christmas**	1 Samuel 2.18–20, 26 Psalm 148 [*or* 148.7–end] Colossians 3.12–17 Luke 2.41–end	Psalm 105.1–11 Isaiah 41.21—42.1 1 John 1.1–7	Psalm 132 Isaiah 61 Galatians 3.27—4.7 *HC* Luke 2.15–21
		Holy Communion	**Morning Prayer**	**Evening Prayer**
Monday	**30 December** W	1 John 2.12–17 Psalm 96.7–10 Luke 2.36–40	Psalms 111, 112, **113** Isaiah 59.1–15*a* John 1.19–28	Psalms **65**, 84 Jonah 2 Colossians 1.15–23
Tuesday	**31 December** W *John Wyclif, reformer, 1384*	1 John 2.18–21 Psalm 96.1, 11–end John 1.1–18	Psalm **102** Isaiah 59.15*b*–end John 1.29–34	Psalms **90**, 148 Jonah 3—4 Colossians 1.24—2.7 *or:* 1st EP of the Naming and Circumcision of Jesus: Psalm 148; Jeremiah 23.1–6; Colossians 2.8–15
		Principal Service	**3rd Service**	**2nd Service**
Wednesday	**1 January** W Naming and Circumcision of Jesus	Numbers 6.22–end Psalm 8 Galatians 4.4–7 Luke 2.15–21	*MP* Psalms 103, 150 Genesis 17.1–13 Romans 2.17–end	*EP* Psalm 115 Deuteronomy 30. [1–10] 11–end Acts 3.1–16
		Holy Communion	**Morning Prayer**	**Evening Prayer**
Thursday	**2 January** W Basil the Great and Gregory of Nazianzus, bishops, teachers of the faith, 379 and 389 (see p.80) *Seraphim, monk, spiritual guide, 1833* *Vedanayagam Samuel Azariah, bishop, evangelist, 1945*	1 John 2.22–28 Psalm 98.1–4 John 1.19–28	Psalm **18.1–30** Isaiah 60.1–12 John 1.35–42	Psalms 45, **46** Ruth 1 Colossians 2.8–end
Friday	**3 January** W	1 John 2.29—3.6 Psalm 98.2–7 John 1.29–34	Psalms **127**, 128, 131 Isaiah 60.13–end John 1.43–end	Psalms **2**, 110 Ruth 2 Colossians 3.1–11

Christmas 2 / Epiphany

If the Epiphany is celebrated on Monday 6 January:

Day	Date	Colour	Holy Communion	Morning Prayer	Evening Prayer
Saturday	**4 January**	*W*	1 John 3.7–10 Psalm 98.1, 8–end John 1.35–42	Psalm **89.1–37** Isaiah 61 John 2.1–12	Psalms 85, **87** Ruth 3 Colossians 3.12—4.1
			Principal Service	**3rd Service**	**2nd Service**
Sunday	**5 January** **2nd Sunday of Christmas**	*W*	Jeremiah 31.7–14 *or* Ecclesiasticus 24.1–12 Psalm 147.13–end *or Canticle:* Wisdom of Solomon 10.15–end Ephesians 1.3–14 John 1.[1–9] 10–18	Psalm 87 Isaiah 12 1 Thessalonians 2.1–8	**1st EP of the Epiphany** Psalms 96, **97** Isaiah 49.1–13 John 4.7–26
Monday	**6 January** **Epiphany**	*Gold or W*	Isaiah 60.1–6 Psalm 72. [1–9] 10–15 Ephesians 3.1–12 Matthew 2.1–12	*MP* Psalms **132**, 113 Jeremiah 31.7–14 John 1.29–34	*EP* Psalms **98**, 100 Baruch 4.36—end of 5 *or* Isaiah 60.1–9 John 2.1–11
			Holy Communion	**Morning Prayer**	**Evening Prayer**
Tuesday	**7 January**	*W*	1 John 3.22—4.6 Psalm 2.7–end Matthew 4.12–17, 23–end	Psalms **99**, 147.1–12 *or* **73** Isaiah 63.7–end 1 John 3	Psalm **118** *or* **74** Baruch 1.15—2.10 *or* Jeremiah 23.1–8 Matthew 20.1–16
Wednesday	**8 January**	*W*	1 John 4.7–10 Psalm 72.1–8 Mark 6.34–44	Psalms **46**, 147.13–end *or* **77** Isaiah 64 1 John 4.7–end	Psalm **145** *or* **119.81–104** Baruch 2.11–end *or* Jeremiah 30.1–17 Matthew 20.17–28
Thursday	**9 January**	*W*	1 John 4.11–18 Psalm 72.1, 10–13 Mark 6.45–52	Psalms 2, **148** *or* **78.1–39*** Isaiah 65.1–16 1 John 5.1–12	Psalms **67**, 72 *or* **78.40–end*** Baruch 3.1–8 *or* Jeremiah 30.18—31.9 Matthew 20.29–end
Friday	**10 January** *William Laud, archbishop, 1645*	*W*	1 John 4.19—5.4 Psalm 72.1, 17–end Luke 4.14–22	Psalms 97, **149** *or* **55** Isaiah 65.17–end 1 John 5.13–end	Psalms 27, **29** *or* **69** Baruch 3.9—4.4 *or* Jeremiah 31.10–17 Matthew 23.1–12
Saturday	**11 January** *Mary Slessor, missionary, 1915*	*W*	1 John 5.5–13 Psalm 147.13–end Luke 5.12–16	Psalms 98, **150** *or* **76**, 79 Isaiah 66.1–11 2 John	**1st EP of the Baptism of Christ:** Psalm 36; Isaiah 61; Titus 2.11–14; 3.4–7

Epiphany

If the Epiphany is celebrated on Sunday 5 January:

Day	Date	Colour	Holy Communion	Morning Prayer	Evening Prayer
Saturday	**4 January**	W	1 John 3.7–10 Psalm 98.1,8–end John 1.35–42	Psalm **89.1–37** Isaiah 61 John 2.1–12	**1st EP of the Epiphany** Psalms 96, **97**; Isaiah 49.1–13; John 4.7–26
			Principal Service	**3rd Service**	**2nd Service**
Sunday	**5 January** **Epiphany**	*Gold or W*	Isaiah 60.1–6 Psalm 72. [1–9] 10–15 Ephesians 3.1–12 Matthew 2.1–12	*MP* Psalms **132**, 113 Jeremiah 31.7–14 John 1.29–34	*EP* Psalms **98**, 100 Baruch 4.36—end of 5 *or* Isaiah 60.1–9 John 2.1–11
			Holy Communion	**Morning Prayer**	**Evening Prayer**
Monday	**6 January**	W	1 John 3.22—4.6 Psalm 2.7–end Matthew 4.12–17, 23–end	Psalms 8, **48** *or* **71** Isaiah 62 John 2.13–end	Psalms 96, **97** *or* **72**, 75 Ruth 4.1–17 Colossians 4.2–end
Tuesday	**7 January**	W	1 John 4.7–10 Psalm 72.1–8 Mark 6.34–44	Psalms **99**, 147.1–12 *or* **73** Isaiah 63.7–end	Psalm **118** *or* **74** Baruch 1.15—2.10 *or* Jeremiah 23.1–8 Matthew 20.1–16
Wednesday	**8 January**	W	1 John 4.11–18 Psalm 72.1, 10–13 Mark 6.45–52	1 John 3 Psalms **46**, 147.13–end *or* **77** Isaiah 64 1 John 4.7–end	Psalms **145** *or* **119.81–104** Baruch 2.11–end *or* Jeremiah 30.1–17 Matthew 20.17–28
Thursday	**9 January**	W	1 John 4.19—5.4 Psalm 72.1, 17–end Luke 4.14–22	Psalms 2, **148** *or* **78.1–39*** Isaiah 65.1–16 1 John 5.1–12	Psalms **67**, 72 *or* **78.40–end*** Baruch 3.1–8 *or* Jeremiah 30.18—31.9 Matthew 20.29–end
Friday	**10 January** *William Laud, archbishop, 1645*	W	1 John 5.5–13 Psalm 147.13–end Luke 5.12–16	Psalms 97, **149** *or* **55** Isaiah 65.17–end 1 John 5.13–end	Psalms 27, **29** *or* **69** Baruch 3.9—4.4 *or* Jeremiah 31.10–17 Matthew 23.1–12
Saturday	**11 January** *Mary Slessor, missionary, 1915*	W	1 John 5.14–end Psalm 149.1–5 John 3.22–30	Psalms 98, **150** *or* **76**, 79 Isaiah 66.1–11 2 John	Psalms **93**, 132 *or* 81, **84** Baruch 4.21–30 *or* Jeremiah 33.14–end Matthew 23.13–28

or: 1st EP of the Baptism of Christ: Psalm 36; Isaiah 61; Titus 2.11–14; 3.4–7

Baptism of Christ (Epiphany 1)

			Principal Service	3rd Service	2nd Service
Sunday	**12 January** Baptism of Christ *1st Sunday of Epiphany*	*Gold or W*	Isaiah 43.1–7 Psalm 29 Acts 8.14–17 Luke 3.15–17, 21–22	Psalm 89.19–29 Isaiah 42.1–9 Acts 19.1–7	Psalms 46, 47 Isaiah 55.1–11 Romans 6.1–11 *HC* Mark 1.4–11
			Holy Communion	**Morning Prayer**	**Evening Prayer**
Monday	**13 January** Hilary, bishop, teacher of the faith, 367 (see p.80) *Kentigern (Mungo), missionary bishop, 603* *George Fox, founder of the Society of Friends (Quakers), 1691* DEL week 1	*W*	Hebrews 1.1–6 Psalm 97.1–2, 6–10 Mark 1.14–20	Psalms **2**, 110 *or* **80**, 82 Amos 1 1 Corinthians 1.1–17	Psalms **34**, 36 *or* **85**, 86 Genesis 1.1–19 Matthew 21.1–17
Tuesday	**14 January**	*W*	Hebrews 2.5–12 Psalm 8 Mark 1.21–28	Psalms 8, **9** *or* 87, **89.1–18** Amos 2 1 Corinthians 1.18–end	Psalms **45**, 46 *or* **89.19–end** Genesis 1.20—2.3 Matthew 21.18–32
Wednesday	**15 January**	*W*	Hebrews 2.14–end Psalm 105.1–9 Mark 1.29–39	Psalms 19, **20** *or* **119.105–128** Amos 3 1 Corinthians 2	Psalms **47**, 48 *or* **91**, 93 Genesis 2.4–end Matthew 21.33–end
Thursday	**16 January**	*W*	Hebrews 3.7–14 Psalm 95.1, 8–end Mark 1.40–end	Psalms **21**, 24 *or* 90, **92** Amos 4 1 Corinthians 3	Psalms **61**, 65 *or* **94** Genesis 3 Matthew 22.1–14
Friday	**17 January** Antony of Egypt, hermit, abbot, 356 (see p.82) *Charles Gore, bishop, founder of the Community of the Resurrection, 1932*	*W*	Hebrews 4.1–5, 11 Psalm 78.3–8 Mark 2.1–12	Psalms **67**, 72 *or* **88** (95) Amos 5.1–17 1 Corinthians 4	Psalm **68** *or* **102** Genesis 4.1–16, 25–26 Matthew 22.15–33
Saturday	**18 January** ***Week of Prayer for Christian Unity: 18–25 January*** *Amy Carmichael, spiritual writer, 1951*	*W*	Hebrews 4.12–end Psalm 19.7–end Mark 2.13–17	Psalms 29, **33** *or* 96, **97**, 100 Amos 5.18–end 1 Corinthians 5	Psalms 84, **85** *or* **104** Genesis 6.1–10 Matthew 22.34–end

Epiphany 2

			Principal Service	3rd Service	2nd Service
Sunday	**19 January** **2nd Sunday of Epiphany**	W	Isaiah 62.1–5 Psalm 36.5–10 1 Corinthians 12.1–11 John 2.1–11	Psalm 145.1–13 Isaiah 49.1–7 Acts 16.11–15	Psalm 96 1 Samuel 3.1–20 Ephesians 4.1–16 *HC* John 1.29–42
			Holy Communion	**Morning Prayer**	**Evening Prayer**
Monday	**20 January** *Richard Rolle, spiritual writer, 1349* DEL week 2	W	Hebrews 5.1–10 Psalm 110.1–4 Mark 2.18–22	Psalms 145, **146** *or* **98**, 99, 101 Amos 6 1 Corinthians 6.1–11	Psalm **71** *or* **105*** (*or* 103) Genesis 6.11—7.10 Matthew 24.1–14
Tuesday	**21 January** Agnes, child martyr, 304 (see p.79)	Wr	Hebrews 6.10–end Psalm 111 Mark 2.23–end	Psalms **132**, 147.1–12 *or* **106*** (*or* 103) Amos 7 1 Corinthians 6.12–end	Psalm **89.1–37** *or* **107*** Genesis 7.11–end Matthew 24.15–28
Wednesday	**22 January** *Vincent of Saragossa, deacon, martyr, 304*	W	Hebrews 7.1–3, 15–17 Psalm 110.1–4 Mark 3.1–6	Psalms **81**, 147.13–end *or* 110, **111**, 112 Amos 8 1 Corinthians 7.1–24	Psalms **97**, 98 *or* **119.129–152** Genesis 8.1–14 Matthew 24.29–end
Thursday	**23 January**	W	Hebrews 7.25—8.6 Psalm 40.7–10, 17–end Mark 3.7–12	Psalms **76**, 148 *or* 113, **115** Amos 9 1 Corinthians 7.25–end	Psalms 99, 100, **111** *or* 114, **116**, 117 Genesis 8.15—9.7 Matthew 25.1–13
Friday	**24 January** Francis de Sales, bishop, teacher of the faith, 1622 (see p.80)	W	Hebrews 8.6–end Psalm 85.7–end Mark 3.13–19	Psalms **27**, 149 *or* **139** Hosea 1.1—2.1 1 Corinthians 8	Psalm **73** *or* 130, 131, 137 Genesis 9.8–19 Matthew 25.14–30 *or:* 1st EP of the Conversion of Paul: Psalm 149; Isaiah 49.1–13; Acts 22.3–16
			Principal Service	**3rd Service**	**2nd Service**
Saturday	**25 January** Conversion of Paul	W	Jeremiah 1.4–10 *or* Acts 9.1–22 Psalm 67 Acts 9.1–22 *or* Galatians 1.11–16*a* Matthew 19.27–end	*MP* Psalms 66, 147.13–end Ezekiel 3.22–end Philippians 3.1–14	*EP* Psalm 119.41–56 Ecclesiasticus 39.1–10 *or* Isaiah 56.1–8 Colossians 1.24—2.7

			Principal Service	3rd Service	2nd Service
Sunday	**26 January** **3rd Sunday of Epiphany**	*W*	Nehemiah 8.1–3, 5–6, 8–10 Psalm 19 [*or* 19.1–6] 1 Corinthians 12.12–31*a* Luke 4.14–21	Psalm 113 Deuteronomy 30.11–15 3 John 1, 5–8	Psalm 33 [*or* 33.1–12] Numbers 9.15–end 1 Corinthians 7.17–24 *HC* Mark 1.21–28
			Holy Communion	**Morning Prayer**	**Evening Prayer**
Monday	**27 January** DEL week 3	*W*	Hebrews 9.15, 24–end Psalm 98.1–7 Mark 3.22–30	Psalms 40, **108** *or* 123, 124, 125, **126** Hosea 2.18—end of 3 1 Corinthians 9.15–end	Psalms **138**, 144 *or* **127**, 128, 129 Genesis 11.27—12.9 Matthew 26.1–16
Tuesday	**28 January** Thomas Aquinas, priest, philosopher, teacher of the faith, 1274 (see p.80)	*W*	Hebrews 10.1–10 Psalm 40.1–4, 7–10 Mark 3.31–end	Psalms 34, **36** *or* **132**, 133 Hosea 4.1–16 1 Corinthians 10.1–13	Psalm **145** *or* (134,) **135** Genesis 13.2–end Matthew 26.17–35
Wednesday	**29 January**	*W*	Hebrews 10.11–18 Psalm 110.1–4 Mark 4.1–20	Psalms 45, **46** *or* **119.153–end** Hosea 5.1–7 1 Corinthians 10.14—11.1	Psalms 21, **29** *or* **136** Genesis 14 Matthew 26.36–46
Thursday	**30 January** Charles, king and martyr, 1649 (see p.79)	*Wr*	Hebrews 10.19–25 Psalm 24.1–6 Mark 4.21–25	Psalms **47**, 48 *or* **143**, 146 Hosea 5.8—6.6 1 Corinthians 11.2–16	Psalms **24**, 33 *or* **138**, 140, 141 Genesis 15 Matthew 26.47–56
Friday	**31 January** *John Bosco, priest, founder of the Salesian Teaching Order, 1888*	*W*	Hebrews 10.32–end Psalm 37.3–6, 40–end Mark 4.26–34	Psalms 61, **65** *or* 142, **144** Hosea 6.7—7.2 1 Corinthians 11.17–end	Psalms **67**, 77 *or* **145** Genesis 16 Matthew 26.57–end
Saturday	**1 February** *Brigid, abbess, c.525*	*W*	Hebrews 11.1–2, 8–19 *Canticle:* Luke 1.69–73 Mark 4.35–end	Psalm **68** *or* **147** Hosea 8 1 Corinthians 12.1–11	**1st EP of the Presentation** Psalm 118 1 Samuel 1.19*b*–end Hebrews 4.11–end

		Principal Service	3rd Service	2nd Service
Sunday	**2 February** *Gold or W* **Presentation of Christ in the Temple** (Candlemas)	Malachi 3.1–5 Psalm 24. [1–6] 7–end Hebrews 2.14–end Luke 2.22–40	*MP* Psalms **48**, 146 Exodus 13.1–16 Romans 12.1–5	*EP* Psalms 122, **132** Haggai 2.1–9 John 2.18–22
		Holy Communion	**Morning Prayer**	**Evening Prayer**
Monday	**3 February** *G* Anskar, archbishop, missionary, 865 (see p.82) Ordinary Time begins today The Collect of 5 before Lent is used DEL week 4	Hebrews 11.32–end Psalm 31.19–end Mark 5.1–20	Psalms **1**, 2, 3 Azariah and Song 1–27 *or* Malachi 1.1, 6–end John 13.1–11	Psalms **4**, 7 Exodus 22.21–27, 23.1–17 Philippians 1.1–11
Tuesday	**4 February** *G* *Gilbert, founder of the Gilbertine Order, 1189*	Hebrews 12.1–4 Psalm 22.25*b*–end Mark 5.21–end	Psalms **5**, 6 (8) Song 28–end *or* Malachi 2.1–16 John 13.12–20	Psalms **9**, 10* Exodus 29.38—30.16 Philippians 1.12–end
Wednesday	**5 February** *G*	Hebrews 12.4–7, 11–15 Psalm 103.1–2, 13–18 Mark 6.1–6*a*	Psalm **119.1–32** Susannah 1–27 *or* Malachi 2.17—3.12 John 13.21–30	Psalms **11**, 12, 13 Leviticus 8 Philippians 2.1–13
Thursday	**6 February** *G* *Martyrs of Japan, 1597*	Hebrews 12.18–19, 21–24 Psalm 48.1–3, 8–10 Mark 6.7–13	Psalms 14, **15**, 16 Susannah 28–end *or* Malachi 3.13—end of 4 John 13.31–end	Psalm **18*** Leviticus 9 Philippians 2.14–end
Friday	**7 February** *G*	Hebrews 13.1–8 Psalm 27.1–6, 9–12 Mark 6.14–29	Psalms 17, **19** Bel and the Dragon *or* Nahum 1 John 14.1–14	Psalm **22** Leviticus 16.2–24 Philippians 3.1—4.1
Saturday	**8 February** *G*	Hebrews 13.15–17, 20–21 Psalm 23 Mark 6.30–34	Psalms 20, 21, **23** Prayer of Manasseh *or* Obadiah John 14.15–end	Psalms **24**, 25 Leviticus 17 Philippians 4.2–end

4 before Lent

			Principal Service	3rd Service	2nd Service
Sunday	**9 February** **4th Sunday before Lent** Proper 1	*G*	Isaiah 6.1–8 [9–end] Psalm 138 1 Corinthians 15.1–11 Luke 5.1–11	Psalms 3, 4 Jeremiah 26.1–16 Acts 3.1–10	Psalms [1] 2 Wisdom 6.1–21 *or* Hosea 1 Colossians 3.1–22 *HC* Matthew 5. 13–20
			Holy Communion	**Morning Prayer**	**Evening Prayer**
Monday	**10 February** *Scholastica, abbess, c.543* DEL week 5	*G*	Genesis 1.1–19 Psalm 104.1, 2, 6–13, 26 Mark 6.53–end	Psalms 27, **30** Joel 1.1–14 John 15.1–11	Psalms 26, **28**, 29 Leviticus 19.1–18, 30–end 1 Timothy 1.1–17
Tuesday	**11 February**	*G*	Genesis 1.20—2.4*a* Psalm 8 Mark 7.1–13	Psalms 32, **36** Joel 1.15–end John 15.12–17	Psalm **33** Leviticus 23.1–22 1 Timothy 1.18—end of 2
Wednesday	**12 February**	*G*	Genesis 2.4*b*–9, 15–17 Psalm 104.11–12, 29–32 Mark 7.14–23	Psalm **34** Joel 2.1–17 John 15.18–end	Psalm **119.33–56** Leviticus 23.23–end 1 Timothy 3
Thursday	**13 February**	*G*	Genesis 2.18–end Psalm 128 Mark 7.24–30	Psalm **37*** Joel 2.18–27 John 16.1–15	Psalms 39, **40** Leviticus 24.1–9 1 Timothy 4
Friday	**14 February** Cyril and Methodius, missionaries, 869 and 885 (see p.82) *Valentine, martyr at Rome, c.269*	*Gw*	Genesis 3.1–8 Psalm 32.1–8 Mark 7.31–end	Psalm **31** Joel 2.28–end John 16.16–22	Psalm **35** Leviticus 25.1–24 1 Timothy 5.1–16
Saturday	**15 February** *Sigfrid, bishop, 1045* *Thomas Bray, priest, founder of SPCK and SPG, 1730*	*G*	Genesis 3.9–end Psalm 90.1–12 Mark 8.1–10	Psalms 41, **42**, 43 Joel 3.1–3, 9–end John 16.23–end	Psalms 45, **46** Numbers 6.1–5, 21–end 1 Timothy 5.17–end

3 before Lent

			Principal Service	3rd Service	2nd Service
Sunday	**16 February** **3rd Sunday before Lent** Proper 2	*G*	Jeremiah 17.5–10 Psalm 1 1 Corinthians 15.12–20 Luke 6.17–26	Psalm 7 Jeremiah 30.1–3, 10–22 Acts 6	Psalms [5] 6 Wisdom 11.21—12.11 *or* Hosea 10.1–8, 12 Galatians 4.8–20 *HC* Matthew 5.21–37
			Holy Communion	**Morning Prayer**	**Evening Prayer**
Monday	**17 February** Janani Luwum, archbishop, martyr, 1977 (see p.79) DEL week 6	*Gr*	Genesis 4.1–15, 25 Psalm 50.1, 8, 16–end Mark 8.11–13	Psalm **44** Ecclesiastes 1 John 17.1–5	Psalms **47**, 49 Genesis 24.1–28 1 Timothy 6.1–10
Tuesday	**18 February**	*G*	Genesis 6.5–8; 7.1–5, 10 Psalm 29 Mark 8.14–21	Psalms **48**, 52 Ecclesiastes 2 John 17.6–19	Psalm **50** Genesis 24.29–end 1 Timothy 6.11–end
Wednesday	**19 February**	*G*	Genesis 8.6–13, 20–end Psalm 116.10–end Mark 8.22–26	Psalm **119.57–80** Ecclesiastes 3.1–15 John 17.20–end	Psalms **59**, 60 (67) Genesis 25.7–11, 19–end 2 Timothy 1.1–14
Thursday	**20 February**	*G*	Genesis 9.1–13 Psalm 102.16–23 Mark 8.27–33	Psalms 56, **57** (63*) Ecclesiastes 3.16—end of 4 John 18.1–11	Psalms 61, **62**, 64 Genesis 26.34—27.40 2 Timothy 1.15—2.13
Friday	**21 February**	*G*	Genesis 11.1–9 Psalm 33.10–15 Mark 8.34—9.1	Psalms **51**, 54 Ecclesiastes 5 John 18.12–27	Psalm **38** Genesis 27.41—end of 28 2 Timothy 2.14–end
Saturday	**22 February**	*G*	Hebrews 11.1–7 Psalm 145.1–10 Mark 9.2–13	Psalm **68** Ecclesiastes 6 John 18.28–end	Psalms 65, **66** Genesis 29.1–30 2 Timothy 3

			Principal Service	3rd Service	2nd Service
Sunday	**23 February** **2nd Sunday before Lent**	*G*	Genesis 2.4*b*–9, 15–end Psalm 65 Revelation 4 Luke 8.22–25	Psalm 104.1–26 Job 28.1–11 Acts 14.8–17	Psalm 147 [*or* 147.13–end] Genesis 1.1—2.3 Matthew 6.25–end
			Holy Communion	**Morning Prayer**	**Evening Prayer**
Monday	**24 February** DEL week 7	*G*	Ecclesiasticus 1.1–10 *or* James 1.1–11 Psalm 93 *or* 119.65–72 Mark 9.14–29	Psalm **71** Ecclesiastes 7.1–14 John 19.1–16	Psalms **72**, 75 Genesis 29.31—30.24 2 Timothy 4.1–8
Tuesday	**25 February**	*G*	Ecclesiasticus 2.1–11 *or* James 1.12–18 Psalm 37.3–6, 27–28 *or* 94.12–18 Mark 9.30–37	Psalm **73** Ecclesiastes 7.15–end John 19.17–30	Psalm **74** Genesis 31.1–24 2 Timothy 4.9–end
Wednesday	**26 February**	*G*	Ecclesiasticus 4.11–19 *or* James 1.19–end Psalm 119.161–168 *or* 15 Mark 9.38–40	Psalm **77** Ecclesiastes 8 John 19.31–end	Psalm **119.81–104** Genesis 31.25—32.2 Titus 1
Thursday	**27 February** George Herbert, priest, poet, 1633 (see p.81)	*Gw*	Ecclesiasticus 5.1–8 *or* James 2.1–9 Psalm 1 *or* 34.1–7 Mark 9.41–end	Psalm **78.1–39*** Ecclesiastes 9 John 20.1–10	Psalm **78.40–end*** Genesis 32.3–30 Titus 2
Friday	**28 February**	*G*	Ecclesiasticus 6.5–17 *or* James 2.14–24, 26 Psalm 119.19–24 *or* 112 Mark 10.1–12	Psalm **55** Ecclesiastes 11.1–8 John 20.11–18	Psalm **69** Genesis 33.1–17 Titus 3
Saturday	**1 March** David, bishop, patron of Wales, c.601 (see p.81)	*Gw*	Ecclesiasticus 17.1–15 *or* James 3.1–10 Psalm 103.13–18 *or* 12.1–7 Mark 10.13–16	Psalms **76**, 79 Ecclesiastes 11.9—end of 12 John 20.19–end	Psalms 81, **84** Genesis 35 Philemon

Sunday next before Lent

Day	Date	Colour	Principal Service	3rd Service	2nd Service
Sunday	**2 March** **Sunday next before Lent**	*G*	Exodus 34.29–end Psalm 99 2 Corinthians 3.12—4.2 Luke 9.28–36 [37–43*a*]	Psalm 2 Exodus 33.17–end 1 John 3.1–3	Psalm 89.1–18 [*or* 89.5–12] Exodus 3.1–6 John 12.27–36*a*
			Holy Communion	**Morning Prayer**	**Evening Prayer**
Monday	**3 March** DEL week 8	*G*	Ecclesiasticus 17.24–29 *or* James 3.13–end Psalm 32.1–8 *or* 19.7–end Mark 10.17–27	Psalms **80**, 82 Jeremiah 1 John 3.1–21	Psalms **85**, 86 Genesis 37.1–11 Galatians 1
Tuesday	**4 March**	*G*	Ecclesiasticus 35.1–12 *or* James 4.1–10 Psalm 50.1–6 *or* 55.7–9, 24 Mark 10.28–31	Psalms 87, **89.1–18** Jeremiah 2.1–13 John 3.22–end	Psalm **89.19–end** Genesis 37.12–end Galatians 2.1–10
			Principal Service	**3rd Service**	**2nd Service**
Wednesday	**5 March** **Ash Wednesday**	*P(La)*	Joel 2.1–2, 12–17 *or* Isaiah 58.1–12 Psalm 51.1–18 2 Corinthians 5.20*b*—6.10 Matthew 6.1–6, 16–21 *or* John 8.1–11	*MP* Psalm **38** Daniel 9.3–6, 17–19 1 Timothy 6.6–19	*EP* Psalm **51** *or* 102 [*or* 102.1–18] Isaiah 1.10–18 Luke 15.11–end
			Holy Communion	**Morning Prayer**	**Evening Prayer**
Thursday	**6 March**	*P(La)*	Deuteronomy 30.15–end Psalm 1 Luke 9.22–25	Psalm **77** *or* 90, **92** Jeremiah 2.14–32 John 4.1–26	Psalm **74** *or* **94** Genesis 39 Galatians 2.11–end
Friday	**7 March** Perpetua, Felicity and companions, martyrs, 203 (see p.79)	*P(La)r*	Isaiah 58.1–9*a* Psalm 51.1–5, 17–18 Matthew 9.14–15	Psalms **3**, 7 *or* **88** (95) Jeremiah 3.6–22 John 4.27–42	Psalm **31** *or* **102** Genesis 40 Galatians 3.1–14
Saturday	**8 March** Edward King, bishop, 1910 (see p.81) *Felix, bishop, 647* *Geoffrey Studdert Kennedy, priest, poet, 1929*	*P(La)w*	Isaiah 58.9*b*–end Psalm 86.1–7 Luke 5.27–32	Psalm **71** *or* 96, **97**, 100 Jeremiah 4.1–18 John 4.43–end	Psalm **73** *or* **104** Genesis 41.1–24 Galatians 3.15–22

Lent 1

			Principal Service	3rd Service	2nd Service
Sunday	**9 March** **1st Sunday of Lent**	*P(La)*	Deuteronomy 26.1–11 Psalm 91.1, 2, 9–end [*or* 91.1–11] Romans 10.8*b*–13 Luke 4.1–13	Psalm 50.1–15 Micah 6.1–8 Luke 5.27–end	Psalm 119.73–88 Jonah 3 Luke 18.9–14
			Holy Communion	**Morning Prayer**	**Evening Prayer**
Monday	**10 March**	*P(La)*	Leviticus 19.1–2, 11–18 Psalm 19.7–end Matthew 25.31–end	Psalms 10, **11** *or* **98**, 99, 101 Jeremiah 4.19–end John 5.1–18	Psalms 12, **13**, 14 *or* **105*** (*or* 103) Genesis 41.25–45 Galatians 3.23—4.7
Tuesday	**11 March**	*P(La)*	Isaiah 55.10–11 Psalm 34.4–6, 21–22 Matthew 6.7–15	Psalm **44** *or* **106*** (*or* 103) Jeremiah 5.1–19 John 5.19–29	Psalms 46, **49** *or* **107*** Genesis 41.46—42.5 Galatians 4.8–20
Wednesday	**12 March** Ember Day	*P(La)*	Jonah 3 Psalm 51.1–5, 17–18 Luke 11.29–32	Psalms **6**, 17 *or* 110, **111**, 112 Jeremiah 5.20–end John 5.30–end	Psalms 9, **28** *or* **119.129–152** Genesis 42.6–17 Galatians 4.21—5.1
Thursday	**13 March**	*P(La)*	Esther 14.1–5, 12–14 *or* Isaiah 55.6–9 Psalm 138 Matthew 7.7–12	Psalms **42**, 43 *or* 113, **115** Jeremiah 6.9–21 John 6.1–15	Psalms 137, 138, **142** *or* 114, **116**, 117 Genesis 42.18–28 Galatians 5.2–15
Friday	**14 March** Ember Day	*P(La)*	Ezekiel 18.21–28 Psalm 130 Matthew 5.20–26	Psalm **22** *or* **139** Jeremiah 6.22–end John 6.16–27	Psalms 54, **55** *or* **130**, 131, 137 Genesis 42.29–end Galatians 5.16–end
Saturday	**15 March** Ember Day	*P(La)*	Deuteronomy 26.16–end Psalm 119.1–8 Matthew 5.43–end	Psalms 59, **63** *or* 120, **121**, 122 Jeremiah 7.1–20 John 6.27–40	Psalms **4**, 16 *or* **118** Genesis 43.1–15 Galatians 6

Lent 2

		Principal Service	3rd Service	2nd Service
Sunday	**16 March** *P(La)* **2nd Sunday of Lent**	Genesis 15.1–12, 17–18 Psalm 27 Philippians 3.17—4.1 Luke 13.31–end	Psalm 119.161–end Genesis 17.1–7, 15–16 Romans 11.13–24	Psalm 135 [*or* 135.1–14] Jeremiah 22.1–9, 13–17 Luke 14.27–33
		Holy Communion	**Morning Prayer**	**Evening Prayer**
Monday	**17 March** *P(La)w* Patrick, bishop, missionary, patron of Ireland, c.460 (see p.82)	Daniel 9.4–10 Psalm 79.8–9, 12, 14 Luke 6.36–38	Psalms 26, **32** *or* 123, 124, 125, **126** Jeremiah 7.21–end John 6.41–51	Psalms 70, **74** *or* **127**, 128, 129 Genesis 43.16–end Hebrews 1
Tuesday	**18 March** *P(La)* *Cyril, bishop, teacher of the faith, 386*	Isaiah 1.10, 16–20 Psalm 50.8, 16–end Matthew 23.1–12	Psalm **50** *or* **132**, 133 Jeremiah 8.1–15 John 6.52–59	Psalms **52**, 53, 54 *or* (134,) **135** Genesis 44.1–17 Hebrews 2.1–9 *or:* 1st EP of Joseph of Nazareth: Psalm 132; Hosea 11.1–9; Luke 2.41–end
		Principal Service	**3rd Service**	**2nd Service**
Wednesday	**19 March** *W* Joseph of Nazareth	2 Samuel 7.4–16 Psalm 89.26–36 Romans 4.13–18 Matthew 1.18–end	*MP* Psalms 25, 147.1–12 Isaiah 11.1–10 Matthew 13.54–end	*EP* Psalms 1, 112 Genesis 50.22–end Matthew 2.13–end
		Holy Communion	**Morning Prayer**	**Evening Prayer**
Thursday	**20 March** *P(La)w* Cuthbert, bishop, missionary, 687 (see p.82)	Jeremiah 17.5–10 Psalm 1 Luke 16.19–end	Psalm **34** *or* **143**, 146 Jeremiah 9.12–24 John 7.1–13	Psalm **71** *or* **138**, 140, 141 Genesis 45.1–15 Hebrews 3.1–6
Friday	**21 March** *P(La)r* Thomas Cranmer, archbishop, Reformation martyr, 1556 (see p.81)	Genesis 37.3–4, 12–13, 17–28 Psalm 105.16–22 Matthew 21.33–43, 45–46	Psalms 40, **41** *or* 142, **144** Jeremiah 10.1–16 John 7.14–24	Psalms **6**, 38 *or* **145** Genesis 45.16–end Hebrews 3.7–end
Saturday	**22 March** *P(La)*	Micah 7.14–15, 18–20 Psalm 103.1–4, 9–12 Luke 15.1–3, 11–end	Psalms 3, **25** *or* **147** Jeremiah 10.17–24 John 7.25–36	Psalms **23**, 27 *or* **148**, 149, 150 Genesis 46.1–7, 28–end Hebrews 4.1–13

		Principal Service	3rd Service	2nd Service
Sunday	**23 March** *P(La)* **3rd Sunday of Lent**	Isaiah 55.1–9 Psalm 63.1–9 1 Corinthians 10.1–13 Luke 13.1–9	Psalms 26, 28 Deuteronomy 6.4–9 John 17.1*a*, 11*b*–19	Psalms 12, 13 Genesis 28.10–19*a* John 1.35–end
		Holy Communion	**Morning Prayer**	**Evening Prayer**
	The following readings may replace those provided for Holy Communion on any day during the Third Week of Lent (except the Feast of the Annunciation of Our Lord): *Exodus 17.1–7; Psalm 95.1–2, 6–end; John 4.5–42*			
Monday	**24 March** *P(La)* *Walter Hilton, mystic, 1396* *Paul Couturier, priest, ecumenist, 1953* *Oscar Romero, archbishop, martyr, 1980*	2 Kings 5.1–15 Psalms 42.1–2; 43.1–4 Luke 4.24–30	Psalms **5**, 7 *or* **1**, 2, 3 Jeremiah 11.1–17 John 7.37–52	**1st EP of The Annunciation of Our Lord to the BVM** Psalm 85 Wisdom 9.1–12 *or* Genesis 3.8–15 Galatians 4.1–5
		Principal Service	**3rd Service**	**2nd Service**
Tuesday	**25 March** *Gold or W* **Annunciation of Our Lord to the Blessed Virgin Mary**	Isaiah 7.10–14 Psalm 40.5–11 Hebrews 10.4–10 Luke 1.26–38	*MP* Psalms 111, 113 1 Samuel 2.1–10 Romans 5.12–end	*EP* Psalms 131, 146 Isaiah 52.1–12 Hebrews 2.5–end
		Holy Communion	**Morning Prayer**	**Evening Prayer**
Wednesday	**26 March** *P(La)* *Harriet Monsell, founder of the Community of St John the Baptist, 1883*	Deuteronomy 4.1, 5–9 Psalm 147.13–end Matthew 5.17–19	Psalm **38** *or* **119.1–32** Jeremiah 13.1–11 John 8.12–30	Psalms 36, **39** *or* **11**, 12, 13 Genesis 49.1–32 Hebrews 6.13–end
Thursday	**27 March** *P(La)*	Jeremiah 7.23–28 Psalm 95.1–2, 6–end Luke 11.14–23	Psalms **56**, 57 *or* 14, **15**, 16 Jeremiah 14 John 8.31–47	Psalms **59**, 60 *or* **18*** Genesis 49.33—end of 50 Hebrews 7.1–10
Friday	**28 March** *P(La)*	Hosea 14 Psalm 81.6–10, 13, 16 Mark 12.28–34	Psalm **22** *or* 17, **19** Jeremiah 15.10–end John 8.48–end	Psalm **69** *or* **22** Exodus 1.1–14 Hebrews 7.11–end
Saturday	**29 March** *P(La)*	Hosea 5.15—6.6 Psalm 51.1–2, 17–end Luke 18.9–14	Psalm **31** *or* 20, **21**, 23 Jeremiah 16.10—17.4 John 9.1–17	Psalms **116**, 130 *or* **24**, 25 Exodus 1.22—2.10 Hebrews 8

Lent 4

			Principal Service	3rd Service	2nd Service
Sunday	**30 March** **4th Sunday of Lent**	*P(La)*	Joshua 5.9–12 Psalm 32 2 Corinthians 5.16–end Luke 15.1–3,11*b*–end	Psalms 84, 85 Genesis 37.3, 4, 12–end 1 Peter 2.16–end	Psalm 30 Prayer of Manasseh *or* Isaiah 40.27—41.13 2 Timothy 4.1–18 *HC* John 11.17–44

For Mothering Sunday:
Exodus 2.1–10 *or* 1 Samuel 1.20–end; Psalm 34.11–20 *or* 127.1–4; 2 Corinthians 1.3–7 *or* Colossians 3.12–17; Luke 2.33–35 *or* John 19.25*b*–27
If the Principal Service readings have been displaced by Mothering Sunday provisions, they may be used at the Second Service.

			Holy Communion	Morning Prayer	Evening Prayer

The following readings may replace those provided for Holy Communion on any day during the Fourth Week of Lent:
Micah 7.7–9; Psalm 27.1, 9–10, 16–17; John 9

			Holy Communion	Morning Prayer	Evening Prayer
Monday	**31 March** *John Donne, priest, poet, 1631*	*P(La)*	Isaiah 65.17–21 Psalm 30.1–5, 8, 11–end John 4.43–end	Psalms 70, **77** *or* 27, **30** Jeremiah 17.5–18 John 9.18–end	Psalms **25**, 28 *or* 26, **28**, 29 Exodus 2.11–22 Hebrews 9.1–14
Tuesday	**1 April** *Frederick Denison Maurice, priest, teacher of the faith, 1872*	*P(La)*	Ezekiel 47.1–9, 12 Psalm 46.1–8 John 5.1–3, 5–16	Psalms 54, **79** *or* 32, **36** Jeremiah 18.1–12 John 10.1–10	Psalms **80**, 82 *or* **33** Exodus 2.23—3.20 Hebrews 9.15–end
Wednesday	**2 April**	*P(La)*	Isaiah 49.8–15 Psalm 145.8–18 John 5.17–30	Psalms 63, **90** *or* **34** Jeremiah 18.13–end John 10.11–21	Psalms 52, **91** *or* **119.33–56** Exodus 4.1–23 Hebrews 10.1–18
Thursday	**3 April**	*P(La)*	Exodus 32.7–14 Psalm 106.19–23 John 5.31–end	Psalms 53, **86** *or* **37*** Jeremiah 19.1–13 John 10.22–end	Psalm **94** *or* 39, **40** Exodus 4.27—6.1 Hebrews 10.19–25
Friday	**4 April**	*P(La)*	Wisdom 2.1, 12–22 *or* Jeremiah 26.8–11 Psalm 34.15–end John 7.1–2, 10, 25–30	Psalm **102** *or* **31** Jeremiah 19.14—20.6 John 11.1–16	Psalms 13, **16** *or* **35** Exodus 6.2–13 Hebrews 10.26–end
Saturday	**5 April**	*P(La)*	Jeremiah 11.18–20 Psalm 7.1–2, 8–10 John 7.40–52	Psalm **32** *or* 41, **42**, 43 Jeremiah 20.7–end John 11.17–27	Psalms **140**, 141, 142 *or* 45, **46** Exodus 7.8–end Hebrews 11.1–16

Day	Date		Principal Service	3rd Service	2nd Service
Sunday	**6 April** **5th Sunday of Lent** *Passiontide begins*	*P(La)*	Isaiah 43.16–21 Psalm 126 Philippians 3.4*b*–14 John 12.1–8	Psalms 111, 112 Isaiah 35 Romans 7.21—8.4	Psalm 35 [*or* 35.1–9] 2 Chronicles 35.1–6, 10–16 Luke 22.1–13
			Holy Communion	**Morning Prayer**	**Evening Prayer**
The following readings may replace those provided for Holy Communion on any day during the Fifth Week of Lent: 2 Kings 4.18–21, 32–37; Psalm 17.1–8, 16; John 11.1–45					
Monday	**7 April**	*P(La)*	Susannah 1–9, 15–17, 19–30, 33–62 [*or* 41*b*–62] *or* Joshua 2.1–14 Psalm 23 John 8.1–11	Psalms **73**, 121 *or* **44** Jeremiah 21.1–10 John 11.28–44	Psalms **26**, 27 *or* **47**, 49 Exodus 8.1–19 Hebrews 11.17–31
Tuesday	**8 April**	*P(La)*	Numbers 21.4–9 Psalm 102.1–3, 16–23 John 8.21–30	Psalms **35**, 123 *or* **48**, 52 Jeremiah 22.1–5, 13–19 John 11.45–end	Psalms **61**, 64 *or* **50** Exodus 8.20–end Hebrews 11.32—12.2
Wednesday	**9 April** *Dietrich Bonhoeffer, Lutheran pastor, martyr, 1945*	*P(La)*	Daniel 3.14–20, 24–25, 28 *Canticle:* Bless the Lord John 8.31–42	Psalms **55**, 124 *or* **119.57–80** Jeremiah 22.20—23.8 John 12.1–11	Psalms 56, **62** *or* **59**, 60 (67) Exodus 9.1–12 Hebrews 12.3–13
Thursday	**10 April** William Law, priest, spiritual writer, 1761 (see p.80) *William of Ockham, friar, philosopher, teacher of the faith, 1347*	*P(La)w*	Genesis 17.3–9 Psalm 105.4–9 John 8.51–end	Psalms **40**, 125 *or* 56, **57** (63*) Jeremiah 23.9–32 John 12.12–19	Psalms 42, **43** *or* 61, **62**, 64 Exodus 9.13–end Hebrews 12.14–end
Friday	**11 April** *George Selwyn, bishop, 1878*	*P(La)*	Jeremiah 20.10–13 Psalm 18.1–6 John 10.31–end	Psalms **22**, 126 *or* **51**, 54 Jeremiah 24 John 12.20–36*a*	Psalm **31** *or* **38** Exodus 10 Hebrews 13.1–16
Saturday	**12 April**	*P(La)*	Ezekiel 37.21–end *Canticle:* Jeremiah 31.10–13 *or* Psalm 121 John 11.45–end	Psalms **23**, 127 *or* **68** Jeremiah 25.1–14 John 12.36*b*–end	Psalms 128, 129, **130** *or* 65, **66** Exodus 11 Hebrews 13.17–end

Holy Week

			Principal Service		3rd Service	2nd Service
Sunday	**13 April** **Palm Sunday**	*R*	*Liturgy of the Palms:* Luke 19.28–40 Psalm 118.1–2,19–end [*or* 118.19–24]	*Liturgy of the Passion:* Isaiah 50.4–9*a* Psalm 31.9–16 [*or* 31.9–18] Philippians 2.5–11 Luke 22.14—end of 23 *or* Luke 23.1–49	Psalms 61, 62 Zechariah 9.9–12 1 Corinthians 2.1–12	Psalm 69.1–20 Isaiah 5.1–7 Luke 20.9–19
			Holy Communion		**Morning Prayer**	**Evening Prayer**
					From the Monday of Holy Week until the Saturday of Easter Week the seasonal psalmody must be used.	
Monday	**14 April** Monday of Holy Week	*R*	Isaiah 42.1–9 Psalm 36.5–11 Hebrews 9.11–15 John 12.1–11		Psalm 41 Lamentations 1.1–12*a* Luke 22.1–23	Psalm 25 Lamentations 2.8–19 Colossians 1.18–23
Tuesday	**15 April** Tuesday of Holy Week	*R*	Isaiah 49.1–7 Psalm 71.1–14 [*or* 71.1–8] 1 Corinthians 1.18–31 John 12.20–36		Psalm 27 Lamentations 3.1–18 Luke 22. [24–38] 39–53	Psalm 55.13–24 Lamentations 3.40–51 Galatians 6.11–end
Wednesday	**16 April** Wednesday of Holy Week	*R*	Isaiah 50.4–9*a* Psalm 70 Hebrews 12.1–3 John 13.21–32		Psalm 102 [*or* 102.1–18] Wisdom 1.16—2.1; 2.12–22 *or* Jeremiah 11.18–20 Luke 22.54–end	Psalm 88 Isaiah 63.1–9 Revelation 14.18—15.4
Thursday	**17 April** **Maundy Thursday**	*R for MP and EP, W for Holy Communion*	Exodus 12.1–4 [5–10] 11–14 Psalm 116.1, 10–end [*or* 116.9–end] 1 Corinthians 11.23–26 John 13.1–17, 31*b*–35		Psalms 42, 43 Leviticus 16.2–24 Luke 23.1–25	Psalm 39 Exodus 11 Ephesians 2.11–18
Friday	**18 April** **Good Friday**	*Hangings removed; R for the Liturgy*	Isaiah 52.13—end of 53 Psalm 22 [*or* 22.1–11 *or* 22.1–21] Hebrews 10.16–25 *or* Hebrews 4.14–16; 5.7–9 John 18.1—end of 19		Psalm 69 Genesis 22.1–18 *A part of John 18 and 19 may be read, if not used at the Principal Service* *or* Hebrews 10.1–10	Psalms 130, 143 Lamentations 5.15–end John 19.38–end *or* Colossians 1.18–23

		Principal Service	3rd Service	2nd Service
Saturday	**19 April** *Hangings removed* **Easter Eve** *These readings are for use at services other than the Easter Vigil.*	Job 14.1–14 *or* Lamentations 3.1–9, 19–24 Psalm 31.1–4, 15–16 [*or* 31.1–5] 1 Peter 4.1–8 Matthew 27.57–end *or* John 19.38–end	Psalm 142 Hosea 6.1–6 John 2.18–22	Psalm 116 Job 19.21–27 1 John 5.5–12
Saturday *or* **Sunday**	**19 April evening** *Gold or W* **20 April morning** *Easter Vigil* *The New Testament readings should be preceded by a minimum of three Old Testament readings.* *The Exodus reading should always be used.*	Genesis 1.1—2.4*a* Genesis 7.1–5, 11–18; 8.6–18; 9.8–13 Genesis 22.1–18 **Exodus 14.10–end; 15.20–21** Isaiah 55.1–11 Baruch 3.9–15, 32—4.4 *or* Proverbs 8.1–8, 19–21; 9.4*b*–6 Ezekiel 36.24–28 Ezekiel 37.1–14 Zephaniah 3.14–end **Romans 6.3–11** **Luke 24.1–12**	Psalm 136.1–9, 23–end Psalm 46 Psalm 16 ***Canticle:* Exodus 15.1*b*–13, 17–18** *Canticle:* Isaiah 12.2–end Psalm 19 Psalms 42, 43 Psalm 143 Psalm 98 **Psalm 114**	
Sunday	**20 April** *Gold or W* **Easter Day**	Acts 10.34–43 † *or* Isaiah 65.17–end Psalm 118.1–2, 14–24 [*or* 118.14–24] 1 Corinthians 15. 19–26 *or* Acts 10.34–43 † John 20.1–18 *or* Luke 24.1–12 † *The reading from Acts must be used as either the first or second reading.*	*MP* Psalms 114, 117 Ezekiel 47.1–12 John 2.13–22	*EP* Psalm 105 *or* 66.1–11 Isaiah 43.1–21 1 Corinthians 15.1–11 *or* John 20.19–23

Easter Week

			Holy Communion	Morning Prayer	Evening Prayer
Monday	**21 April** Monday of Easter Week	W	Acts 2.14, 22–32 Psalm 16.1–2, 6–end Matthew 28.8–15	Psalms **111**, 117, 146 Song of Solomon 1.9—2.7 Mark 16.1–8	Psalm **135** Exodus 12.1–14 1 Corinthians 15.1–11
Tuesday	**22 April** Tuesday of Easter Week	W	Acts 2.36–41 Psalm 33.4–5, 18–end John 20.11–18	Psalms **112**, 147.1–12 Song of Solomon 2.8–end Luke 24.1–12	Psalm **136** Exodus 12.14–36 1 Corinthians 15.12–19
Wednesday	**23 April** Wednesday of Easter Week	W	Acts 3.1–10 Psalm 105.1–9 Luke 24.13–35	Psalms **113**, 147.13–end Song of Solomon 3 Matthew 28.16–end	Psalm **105** Exodus 12.37–end 1 Corinthians 15.20–28
Thursday	**24 April** Thursday of Easter Week	W	Acts 3.11–end Psalm 8 Luke 24.35–48	Psalms **114**, 148 Song of Solomon 5.2—6.3 Luke 7.11–17	Psalm **106** Exodus 13.1–16 1 Corinthians 15.29–34
Friday	**25 April** Friday of Easter Week	W	Acts 4.1–12 Psalm 118.1–4, 22–26 John 21.1–14	Psalms **115**, 149 Song of Solomon 7.10—8.4 Luke 8.41–end	Psalm **107** Exodus 13.17—14.14 1 Corinthians 15.35–50
Saturday	**26 April** Saturday of Easter Week	W	Acts 4.13–21 Psalm 118.1–4, 14–21 Mark 16.9–15	Psalms **116**, 150 Song of Solomon 8.5–7 John 11.17–44	Psalm **145** Exodus 14.15–end 1 Corinthians 15.51–end

Day	Date		Principal Service	3rd Service	2nd Service
Sunday	**27 April** **2nd Sunday of Easter**	*W*	[Exodus 14.10–end; 15.20, 21] Acts 5.27–32 † Psalm 118.14–end *or* Psalm 150 Revelation 1.4–8 John 20.19–end † *The reading from Acts must be used as either the first or second reading.*	Psalm 136.1–16 Exodus 12.1–13 1 Peter 1.3–12	Psalm 16 Isaiah 52.13—53.12 *or* 53.1–6, 9–12 Luke 24.13–35 *or:* 1st EP of George, martyr, patron of England: Psalms 111, 116; Jeremiah 15.15–end; Hebrews 11.32—12.2
Monday	**28 April** George, martyr, patron of England, c.304 *(transferred from 23 April)*	*R*	1 Maccabees 2.59–64 *or* Revelation 12.7–12 Psalm 126 2 Timothy 2.3–13 John 15.18–21	*MP* Psalms 5, 146 Joshua 1.1–9 Ephesians 6.10–20	*EP* Psalms 3, 11 Isaiah 43.1–7 John 15.1–8 *or:* 1st EP of Mark the Evangelist: Psalm 19; Isaiah 52.7–10; Mark 1.1–15
Tuesday	**29 April** *(transferred from 25 April)* Mark the Evangelist	*R*	Proverbs 15.28–end *or* Acts 15.35–end Psalm 119.9–16 Ephesians 4.7–16 Mark 13.5–13	*MP* Psalms 37.23–end, 148 Isaiah 62.6–10 *or* Ecclesiasticus 51.13–end Acts 12.25—13.13	*EP* Psalm 45 Ezekiel 1.4–14 2 Timothy 4.1–11
			Holy Communion	**Morning Prayer**	**Evening Prayer**
Wednesday	**30 April** *Pandita Mary Ramabai, translator, 1922*	*W*	Acts 5.17–26 Psalm 34.1–8 John 3.16–21	Psalms 16, **30** *or* **119.1–32** Deuteronomy 3.18–end John 20.19–end	Psalm **33** *or* **11**, 12, 13 Exodus 16.11–end Colossians 2.1–15 *or:* 1st EP of Philip and James, Apostles: Psalm 25; Isaiah 40.27–end; John 12.20–26
			Principal Service	**3rd Service**	**2nd Service**
Thursday	**1 May** Philip and James, Apostles	*R*	Isaiah 30.15–21 Psalm 119.1–8 Ephesians 1.3–10 John 14.1–14	*MP* Psalms 139, 146 Proverbs 4.10–18 James 1.1–12	*EP* Psalm 149 Job 23.1–12 John 1.43–end
			Holy Communion	**Morning Prayer**	**Evening Prayer**
Friday	**2 May** Athanasius, bishop, teacher of the faith, 373 (see p.80)	*W*	Acts 5.34–42 Psalm 27.1–5, 16–17 John 6.1–15	Psalms 57, **61** *or* 17, **19** Deuteronomy 4.15–31 John 21.15–19	Psalm **118** *or* **22** Exodus 18.1–12 Colossians 3.12—4.1
Saturday	**3 May**	*W*	Acts 6.1–7 Psalm 33.1–5, 18–19 John 6.16–21	Psalms 63, **84** *or* 20, 21, **23** Deuteronomy 4.32–40 John 21.20–end	Psalm **66** *or* **24**, 25 Exodus 18.13–end Colossians 4.2–end

Day	Date		Principal Service	3rd Service	2nd Service
Sunday	**4 May** **3rd Sunday of Easter**	*W*	[Zephaniah 3.14–end] Acts 9.1–6 [7–20] † Psalm 30 Revelation 5.11–end John 21.1–19 † *The reading from Acts must be used as either the first or second reading.*	Psalm 80.1–8 Exodus 15.1–2, 9–18 John 10.1–19	Psalm 86 Isaiah 38.9–20 John 11. [17–26] 27–44
			Holy Communion	**Morning Prayer**	**Evening Prayer**
Monday	**5 May**	*W*	Acts 6.8–15 Psalm 119.17–24 John 6.22–29	Psalms **96**, 97 *or* 27, **30** Deuteronomy 5.1–22 Ephesians 1.1–14	Psalms **61**, 65 *or* 26, **28**, 29 Exodus 19 Luke 1.1–25
Tuesday	**6 May**	*W*	Acts 7.51—8.1*a* Psalm 31.1–5, 16 John 6.30–35	Psalms **98**, 99, 100 *or* 32, **36** Deuteronomy 5.22–end Ephesians 1.15–end	Psalm **71** *or* **33** Exodus 20.1–21 Luke 1.26–38
Wednesday	**7 May**	*W*	Acts 8.1*b*–8 Psalm 66.1–6 John 6.35–40	Psalm **105** *or* **34** Deuteronomy 6 Ephesians 2.1–10	Psalms 67, **72** *or* **119.33–56** Exodus 24 Luke 1.39–56
Thursday	**8 May** Julian of Norwich, spiritual writer, c.1417 (see p.82)	*W*	Acts 8.26–end Psalm 66.7–8, 14–end John 6.44–51	Psalm **136** *or* **37*** Deuteronomy 7.1–11 Ephesians 2.11–end	Psalm **73** *or* 39, **40** Exodus 25.1–22 Luke 1.57–end
Friday	**9 May**	*W*	Acts 9.1–20 Psalm 117 John 6.52–59	Psalm **107** *or* **31** Deuteronomy 7.12–end Ephesians 3.1–13	Psalm **77** *or* **35** Exodus 28.1–4*a*, 29–38 Luke 2.1–20
Saturday	**10 May**	*W*	Acts 9.31–42 Psalm 116.10–15 John 6.60–69	Psalms 108, **110**, 111 *or* 41, **42**, 43 Deuteronomy 8 Ephesians 3.14–end	Psalms 23, **27** *or* 45, **46** Exodus 29.1–9 Luke 2.21–40

			Principal Service	3rd Service	2nd Service
Sunday	**11 May** **4th Sunday of Easter**	W	[Genesis 7.1–5, 11–18; 8.6–18; 9.8–13] Acts 9.36–end † Psalm 23 Revelation 7.9–end John 10.22–30 *† The reading from Acts must be used as either the first or second reading.*	Psalm 146 1 Kings 17.17–end Luke 7.11–23	Psalms 113, 114 Isaiah 63.7–14 Luke 24.36–49
			Holy Communion	**Morning Prayer**	**Evening Prayer**
Monday	**12 May** *Gregory Dix, priest, monk, scholar, 1952*	W	Acts 11.1–18 Psalms 42.1–2; 43.1–4 John 10.1–10 (*or* 11–18)	Psalm **103** *or* **44** Deuteronomy 9.1–21 Ephesians 4.1–16	Psalms 112, 113, **114** *or* **47**, 49 Exodus 32.1–14 Luke 2.41–end
Tuesday	**13 May**	W	Acts 11.19–26 Psalm 87 John 10.22–30	Psalm **139** *or* **48**, 52 Deuteronomy 9.23—10.5 Ephesians 4.17–end	Psalms 115, **116** *or* **50** Exodus 32.15–34 Luke 3.1–14 *or:* 1st EP of Matthias the Apostle: Psalm 147; Isaiah 22.15–22; Philippians 3.13*b*—4.1
			Principal Service	**3rd Service**	**2nd Service**
Wednesday	**14 May** Matthias the Apostle	*R*	Isaiah 22.15–end *or* Acts 1.15–end Psalm 15 Acts 1.15–end *or* 1 Corinthians 4.1–7 John 15.9–17	*MP* Psalms 16, 147.1–12 1 Samuel 2.27–35 Acts 2.37–end	*EP* Psalm 80 1 Samuel 16.1–13*a* Matthew 7.15–27
			Holy Communion	**Morning Prayer**	**Evening Prayer**
Thursday	**15 May**	W	Acts 13.13–25 Psalm 89.1–2, 20–26 John 13.16–20	Psalm **118** *or* 56, **57** (63*) Deuteronomy 11.8–end Ephesians 5.15–end	Psalms 81, **85** *or* 61, **62**, 64 Exodus 34.1–10, 27–end Luke 4.1–13
Friday	**16 May** *Caroline Chisholm, social reformer, 1877*	W	Acts 13.26–33 Psalm 2 John 14.1–6	Psalm **33** *or* **51**, 54 Deuteronomy 12.1–14 Ephesians 6.1–9	Psalms **36**, 40 *or* **38** Exodus 35.20—36.7 Luke 4.14–30
Saturday	**17 May**	W	Acts 13.44–end Psalm 98.1–5 John 14.7–14	Psalm **34** *or* **68** Deuteronomy 15.1–18 Ephesians 6.10–end	Psalms **84**, 86 *or* 65, **66** Exodus 40.17–end Luke 4.31–37

Day	Date	Colour	Principal Service	3rd Service	2nd Service
Sunday	**18 May** **5th Sunday of Easter**	W	[Baruch 3.9–15, 32—4.4 *or* Genesis 22.1–18] Acts 11.1–18 † Psalm 148 [*or* 148.1–6] Revelation 21.1–6 John 13.31–35 † *The reading from Acts must be used as either the first or second reading.*	Psalm 16 2 Samuel 7.4–13 Acts 2.14*a*, 22–32 [33–36]	Psalm 98 Daniel 6. [1–5] 6–23 Mark 15.46—16.8
			Holy Communion	**Morning Prayer**	**Evening Prayer**
Monday	**19 May** Dunstan, archbishop, monastic reformer, 988 (see p.81)	W	Acts 14.5–18 Psalm 118.1–3, 14–15 John 14.21–26	Psalm **145** *or* **71** Deuteronomy 16.1–20 1 Peter 1.1–12	Psalm **105** *or* **72**, 75 Numbers 9.15–end; 10.33–end Luke 4.38–end
Tuesday	**20 May** Alcuin, deacon, abbot, 804 (see p.82)	W	Acts 14.19–end Psalm 145.10–end John 14.27–end	Psalms **19**, 147.1–12 *or* **73** Deuteronomy 17.8–end 1 Peter 1.13–end	Psalms 96, **97** *or* **74** Numbers 11.1–33 Luke 5.1–11
Wednesday	**21 May** *Helena, protector of the Holy Places, 330*	W	Acts 15.1–6 Psalm 122.1–5 John 15.1–81	Psalms **30**, 147.13–end *or* **77** Deuteronomy 18.9–end Peter 2.1–10	Psalms 98, **99**, 100 *or* **119.81–104** Numbers 12 Luke 5.12–26
Thursday	**22 May**	W	Acts 15.7–21 Psalm 96.1–3, 7–10 John 15.9–11	Psalms **57**, 148 *or* **78.1–39*** Deuteronomy 19 1 Peter 2.11–end	Psalm **104** *or* **78.40–end*** Numbers 13.1–3, 17–end Luke 5.27–end
Friday	**23 May**	W	Acts 15.22–31 Psalm 57.8–end John 15.12–17	Psalms **138**, 149 *or* **55** Deuteronomy 21.22—22.8 1 Peter 3.1–12	Psalm **66** *or* **69** Numbers 14.1–25 Luke 6.1–11
Saturday	**24 May** John and Charles Wesley, evangelists, hymn writers, 1791 and 1788 (see p.81)	W	Acts 16.1–10 Psalm 100 John 15.18–21	Psalms **146**, 150 *or* **76**, 79 Deuteronomy 24.5–end 1 Peter 3.13–end	Psalm **118** *or* 81, **84** Numbers 14.26–end Luke 6.12–26

Easter 6

			Principal Service	3rd Service	2nd Service
Sunday	**25 May** **6th Sunday of Easter**	*W*	[Ezekiel 37.1–14] Acts 16.9–15 † Psalm 67 Revelation 21.10, 22—22.5 John 14.23–29 *or* John 5.1–9 † *The reading from Acts must be used as either the first or second reading.*	Psalm 40.1–9 Genesis 1.26–28 [29–end] Colossians 3.1–11	Psalms 126, 127 Zephaniah 3.14–end Matthew 28.1–10, 16–end
			Holy Communion	**Morning Prayer**	**Evening Prayer**
Monday	**26 May** Rogation Day Augustine, archbishop, 605 (see p.81) *John Calvin, reformer, 1564* *Philip Neri, founder of the Oratorians, spiritual guide, 1595*	*W*	Acts 16.11–15 Psalm 149.1–5 John 15.26—16.4	Psalms **65**, 67 *or* **80**, 82 Deuteronomy 26 1 Peter 4.1–11	Psalms **121**, 122, 123 *or* **85**, 86 Numbers 16.1–35 Luke 6.27–38
Tuesday	**27 May** Rogation Day	*W*	Acts 16.22–34 Psalm 138 John 16.5–11	Psalms 124, 125, **126**, 127 *or* 87, **89.1–18** Deuteronomy 28.1–14 1 Peter 4.12–end	Psalms **128**, 129, 130, 131 *or* **89.19–end** Numbers 16.36–end Luke 6.39–end
Wednesday	**28 May** Rogation Day *Lanfranc, monk, archbishop, scholar, 1089*	*W*	Acts 17.15, 22—18.1 Psalm 148.1–2, 11–end John 16.12–15	Psalms **132**, 133 *or* **119.105–128** Deuteronomy 28.58–end 1 Peter 5	**1st EP of Ascension Day** Psalms 15, 24 2 Samuel 23.1–5 Colossians 2.20—3.4

			Principal Service	3rd Service	2nd Service
Thursday	**29 May** **Ascension Day**	*W*	Acts 1.1–11 † *or* Daniel 7.9–14 Psalm 47 *or* Psalm 93 Ephesians 1.15–end *or* Acts 1.1–11 † Luke 24.44–end † *The reading from Acts must be used as either the first or second reading.*	*MP* Psalm 110 Isaiah 52.7–end Hebrews 7.[11–25] 26–end	*EP* Psalm 8 Song of the Three 29–37 *or* 2 Kings 2.1–15 Revelation 5 *HC* Matthew 28.16–end

*The nine days after Ascension Day until the eve of Pentecost are observed as days of prayer and preparation for the celebration of the outpouring of the Holy Spirit. From 30 May–7 June, in preparation for the Day of Pentecost, an alternative sequence of daily readings for use at the one of the offices is marked with an asterisk *.*

			Holy Communion	Morning Prayer	Evening Prayer
Friday	**30 May** Josephine Butler, social reformer, 1906 (see p.83) *Joan of Arc, visionary, 1431* *Apolo Kivebulaya, priest, evangelist, 1933*	*W*	Acts 18.9–18 Psalm 47.1–6 John 16.20–23	Psalms 20, **81** *or* **88** (95) Deuteronomy 29.2–15 1 John 1.1—2.6 **Exodus 35.30—36.1; Galatians 5.13–end*	Psalm **145** *or* **102** Numbers 20.1–13 Luke 7.11–17

or: 1st EP of the Visit of the BVM to Elizabeth: Psalm 45; Song of Solomon 2.8–14; Luke 1.26–38

			Principal Service	3rd Service	2nd Service
Saturday	**31 May** Visit of the Blessed Virgin Mary to Elizabeth	*W*	Zephaniah 3.14–18 Psalm 113 Romans 12.9–16 Luke 1.38–49 [50–56]	*MP* Psalms 85, 150 1 Samuel 2.1–10 Mark 3.31–end	*EP* Psalms 122, 127, 128 Zechariah 2.10–end John 3.25–30

Easter 7

		Principal Service	3rd Service	2nd Service
Sunday	**1 June** *W* **7th Sunday of Easter** *Sunday after Ascension Day*	[Ezekiel 36.24–28] Acts 16.16–34 † Psalm 97 Revelation 22.12–14, 16–17, 20–end John 17.20–end † *The reading from Acts must be used as either the first or second reading.*	Psalm 99 Deuteronomy 34 Luke 24.44–end *or* Acts 1.1–8	Psalm 68 [*or* 68.1–13, 18–19] Isaiah 44.1–8 Ephesians 4.7–16 *HC* Luke 24.44–end
		Holy Communion	**Morning Prayer**	**Evening Prayer**
Monday	**2 June** *W*	Acts 19.1–8 Psalm 68.1–6 John 16.29–end	Psalms **93**, 96, 97 *or* **98**, 99, 101 Deuteronomy 31.1–13 1 John 2.18–end **Numbers 27.15–end; 1 Corinthians 3*	Psalm **18** *or* **105*** (*or* 103) Numbers 22.1–35 Luke 7.36–end
Tuesday	**3 June** *W* *Martyrs of Uganda, 1885–7, 1977*	Acts 20.17–27 Psalm 68.9–10, 18–19 John 17.1–11	Psalms 98, **99**, 100 *or* **106*** (*or* 103) Deuteronomy 31.14–29 1 John 3.1–10 **1 Samuel 10.1–10; 1 Corinthians 12.1–13*	Psalm **68** *or* **107*** Numbers 22.36—23.12 Luke 8.1–15
Wednesday	**4 June** *W* *Petroc, abbot, 6th cent.*	Acts 20.28–end Psalm 68.27–28, 32–end John 17.11–19	Psalms 2, **29** *or* 110, **111**, 112 Deuteronomy 31.30—32.14 1 John 3.11–end **1 Kings 19.1–18; Matthew 3.13–end*	Psalms 36, **46** *or* **119.129–152** Numbers 23.13–end Luke 8.16–25
Thursday	**5 June** *Wr* Boniface (Wynfrith), bishop, martyr, 754 (see p.79)	Acts 22.30; 23.6–11 Psalm 16.1, 5–end John 17.20–end	Psalms **24**, 72 *or* 113, **115** Deuteronomy 32.15–47 1 John 4.1–6 **Ezekiel 11.14–20; Matthew 9.35—10.20*	Psalm **139** *or* 114, **116**, 117 Numbers 24 Luke 8.26–39
Friday	**6 June** *W* *Ini Kopuria, founder of the Melanesian Brotherhood, 1945*	Acts 25.13–21 Psalm 103.1–2, 11–12, 19–20 John 21.15–19	Psalms **28**, 30 *or* **139** Deuteronomy 33 1 John 4.7–end **Ezekiel 36.22–28; Matthew 12.22–32*	Psalm **147** *or* **130**, 131, 137 Numbers 27.12–end Luke 8.40–end
Saturday	**7 June** *W*	Acts 28.16–20, 30–end Psalm 11.4–end John 21.20–end	Psalms 42, **43** *or* 120, **121**, 122 Deuteronomy 32.48–end, 34 1 John 5 **Micah 3.1–8; Ephesians 6.10–20*	**1st EP of Pentecost** Psalm **48** Deuteronomy 16.9–15 John 7:37–39

Pentecost / Ordinary Time

Day	Date	Colour	Principal Service	3rd Service	2nd Service
Sunday	**8 June** **Pentecost** *Whit Sunday*	*R*	Acts 2.1–21 † *or* Genesis 11.1–9 Psalm 104.26–36, 37*b* [*or* 104.26–end] Romans 8.14–17 *or* Acts 2.1–21 † John 14.8–17 [25–27] † *The reading from Acts must be used as either the first or second reading.*	*MP* Psalms 36.5–10; 150 Isaiah 40.12–23 *or* Wisdom 9.9–17 1 Corinthians 2.6–end	*EP* Psalm 33.1–12 Exodus 33.7–20 2 Corinthians 3.4–end *HC* John 16.4*b*–15
			Holy Communion	**Morning Prayer**	**Evening Prayer**
Monday	**9 June** Columba, abbot, missionary, 597 (see p.82) *Ephrem, deacon, hymn writer, teacher of the faith, 373* Ordinary Time resumes today DEL week 10	*Gw*	2 Corinthians 1.1–7 Psalm 34.1–8 Matthew 5.1–12	Psalms 123, 124, 125, **126** Job 1 Romans 1.1–17	Psalms **127**, 128, 129 Joshua 1 Luke 9.18–27
Tuesday	**10 June**	*G*	2 Corinthians 1.18–22 Psalm 119.129–136 Matthew 5.13–16	Psalms **132**, 133 Job 2 Romans 1.18–end	Psalms (134), **135** Joshua 2 Luke 9.28–36 *or:* 1st EP of Barnabas the Apostle: Psalms 1, 15; Isaiah 42.5–12; Acts 14.8–end
			Principal Service	**3rd Service**	**2nd Service**
Wednesday	**11 June** Barnabas the Apostle	*R*	Job 29.11–16 *or* Acts 11.19–end Psalm 112 Acts 11.19–end *or* Galatians 2.1–10 John 15.12–17	*MP* Psalms 100, 101, 117 Jeremiah 9.23–24 Acts 4.32–end	*EP* Psalm 147 Ecclesiastes 12.9–end *or* Tobit 4.5–11
			Holy Communion	**Morning Prayer**	**Evening Prayer**
Thursday	**12 June**	*G*	2 Corinthians 3.15—4.1, 3–6 Psalm 78.36–40 Matthew 5.20–26	Psalms **143**, 146 Job 4 Romans 2.17–end	Psalms **138**, 140, 141 Joshua 4.1—5.1 Luke 9.51–end
Friday	**13 June**	*G*	2 Corinthians 4.7–15 Psalm 99 Matthew 5.27–32	Psalms 142, **144** Job 5 Romans 3.1–20	Psalm **145** Joshua 5.2–end Luke 10.1–16
Saturday	**14 June** *Richard Baxter, puritan divine, 1691*	*G*	2 Corinthians 5.14–end Psalm 103.1–12 Matthew 5.33–37	Psalm **147** Job 6 Romans 3.21–end	**1st EP of Trinity Sunday** Psalms 97, 98 Isaiah 40.12–end Mark 1.1–13

Day	Date	Colour	Principal Service	3rd Service	2nd Service
Sunday	**15 June** **Trinity Sunday**	*Gold or W*	Proverbs 8.1–4, 22–31 Psalm 8 Romans 5.1–5 John 16.12–15	*MP* Psalm 29 Isaiah 6.1–8 Revelation 4	*EP* Psalm 73.1–3, 16–end Exodus 3.1–15 John 3.1–17
			Holy Communion	**Morning Prayer**	**Evening Prayer**
Monday	**16 June** Richard, bishop, 1253 (see p.81) *Joseph Butler, bishop, philosopher, 1752* DEL week 11	*Gw*	2 Corinthians 6.1–10 Psalm 98 Matthew 5.38–42	Psalms **1**, 2, 3 Job 7 Romans 4.1–12	Psalms **4**, 7 Joshua 7.1–15 Luke 10.25–37
Tuesday	**17 June** *Samuel and Henrietta Barnett, social reformers, 1913 and 1936*	*G*	2 Corinthians 8.1–9 Psalm 146 Matthew 5.43–end	Psalms **5**, 6 (8) Job 8 Romans 4.13–end	Psalms **9**, 10* Joshua 7.16–end Luke 10.38–end
Wednesday	**18 June** *Bernard Mizeki, martyr, 1896*	*G*	2 Corinthians 9.6–11 Psalm 112 Matthew 6.1–6, 16–18	Psalm **119.1–32** Job 9 Romans 5.1–11	Psalms **11**, 12, 13 Joshua 8.1–29 Luke 11.1–13
				or: 1st EP of Corpus Christi: Psalms 110, 111; Exodus 16.2–15; John 6.22–35	
			Principal Service	**3rd Service**	**2nd Service**
Thursday	**19 June** Day of Thanksgiving for the Institution of the Holy Communion (Corpus Christi)	*W*	Genesis 14.18–20 Psalm 116.10–end 1 Corinthians 11.23–26 John 6.51–58	*MP* Psalm 147 Deuteronomy 8.2–16 1 Corinthians 10.1–17	*EP* Psalms 23, 42, 43 Proverbs 9.1–5 Luke 9.11–17
	Alternatively Corpus Christi may be kept as a Lesser Festival, and either these readings or those given below may be used.				
			Holy Communion	**Morning Prayer**	**Evening Prayer**
or **Thursday**	**19 June** Day of Thanksgiving for the Institution of the Holy Communion (Corpus Christi) *Sundar Singh, sadhu (holy man), evangelist, teacher of the faith, 1929*	*Gw*	2 Corinthians 11.1–11 Psalm 111 Matthew 6.7–15	Psalms 14, **15**, 16 Job 10 Romans 5.12–end	Psalm **18*** Joshua 8.30–end Luke 11.14–28
Friday	**20 June**	*G*	2 Corinthians 11.18, 21*b*–30 Psalm 34.1–6 Matthew 6.19–23	Psalms 17, **19** Job 11 Romans 6.1–14	Psalm **22** Joshua 9.3–26 Luke 11.29–36
Saturday	**21 June**	*G*	2 Corinthians 12.1–10 Psalm 89.20–33 Matthew 6.24–end	Psalms 20, 21, **23** Job 12 Romans 6.15–end	Psalms **24**, 25 Joshua 10.1–15 Luke 11.37–end

Day	Date	Principal Service	3rd Service	2nd Service
Sunday	**22 June** *G* **1st Sunday after Trinity** Proper 7	*Continuous:* 1 Kings 19.1–4 [5–7] 8–15*a* Psalms 42, 43 [*or* 42 *or* 43] *Related:* Isaiah 65.1–9 Psalm 22.19–28 Galatians 3.23–end Luke 8.26–39	Psalm 55.1–16,18–21 Deuteronomy 11.1–15 Acts 27.1–12	Psalms [50] 57 Genesis 24.1–27 Mark 5.21–end
		Holy Communion	**Morning Prayer**	**Evening Prayer**
Monday	**23 June** *Gw* Etheldreda, abbess, c.678 (see p.82) DEL week 12	Genesis 12.1–9 Psalm 33.12–end Matthew 7.1–5	Psalms 27, **30** Job 13 Romans 7.1–6	Psalms 26, **28**, 29 Joshua 14 Luke 12.1–12 *or:* 1st EP of the Birth of John the Baptist: Psalm 71; Judges 13.2–7, 24–end; Luke 1.5–25
		Principal Service	**3rd Service**	**2nd Service**
Tuesday	**24 June** *W* Birth of John the Baptist	Isaiah 40.1–11 Psalm 85.7–end Acts 13.14*b*–26 *or* Galatians 3.23–end Luke 1.57–66, 80	*MP* Psalms 50, 149 Ecclesiasticus 48.1–10 *or* Malachi 3.1–6 Luke 3.1–17	*EP* Psalms 80, 82 Malachi 4 Matthew 11.2–19
		Holy Communion	**Morning Prayer**	**Evening Prayer**
Wednesday	**25 June** *G* Ember Day	Genesis 15.1–12, 17–18 Psalm 105.1–9 Matthew 7.15–20	Psalm **34** Job 15 Romans 8.1–11	Psalm **119.33–56** Joshua 22.9–end Luke 12.22–31
Thursday	**26 June** *G*	Genesis 16.1–12, 15–16 Psalm 106.1–5 Matthew 7.21–end	Psalm **37*** Job 16.1—17.2 Romans 8.12–17	Psalms 39, **40** Joshua 23 Luke 12.32–40
Friday	**27 June** *G* *Cyril, bishop, teacher of the faith, 444* Ember Day	Genesis 17.1, 9–10, 15–22 Psalm 128 Matthew 8.1–4	Psalm **31** Job 17.3–end Romans 8.18–30	Psalm **35** Joshua 24.1–28 Luke 12.41–48
Saturday	**28 June** *Gw* Irenaeus, bishop, teacher of the faith, c.200 (see p.80) Ember Day	Genesis 18.1–15 *Canticle:* Luke 1.46*b*–55 Matthew 8.5–17	Psalms 41, **42**, 43 Job 18 Romans 8.31–end	Psalms 45, **46** Joshua 24.29–end Luke 12.49–end

or, if Peter and Paul, Apostles *is celebrated on Sunday 29 June:* 1st EP of Peter and Paul, Apostles [*or* †Peter the Apostle alone]: Psalms 66, 67; Ezekiel 3.4–11; Galatians 1.13—2.8 [†Acts 9.32–end]

Peter and Paul / Trinity 2

If Peter and Paul, Apostles is celebrated on Sunday 29 June:

		Principal Service		3rd Service	2nd Service
Sunday	**29 June** *R* Peter and Paul, Apostles *or* Peter the Apostle *R*	*Peter and Paul:* Zechariah 4.1–6*a*, 10*b*–end *or* Acts 12.1–11 Psalm 125 Acts 12.1–11 *or* 2 Timothy 4.6–8, 17–18 Matthew 16.13–19	*Peter alone:* Ezekiel 3.22–end *or* Acts 12.1–11 Psalm 125 Acts 12.1–11 *or* 1 Peter 2.19–end Matthew 16.13–19	*MP* Psalms 71, 113 Isaiah 49.1–6 Acts 11.1–18	*EP* Psalms 124, 138 Ezekiel 34.11–16 John 21.15–22
		Holy Communion		**Morning Prayer**	**Evening Prayer**
Monday	**30 June** *G* DEL week 13	Genesis 18.16–end Psalm 103.6–17 Matthew 8.18–22		Psalm **44** Job 19 Romans 9.1–18	Psalms **47**, 49 Judges 2 Luke 13.1–9

If Peter and Paul, Apostles is transferred to Monday 30 June:

		Principal Service		3rd Service	2nd Service
Sunday	**29 June** *G* **2nd Sunday after Trinity** Proper 8	*Continuous:* 2 Kings 2.1–2, 6–14 Psalm 77.1–2, 11–end *or* 77.11–end] Galatians 5.1, 13–25 Luke 9.51–end	*Related:* 1 Kings 19.15–16, 19–end Psalm 16	Psalm 64 Deuteronomy 15.1–11 Acts 27. [13–32] 33–end	Psalms [59.1–6, 18–end] 60 Genesis 27.1–40 Mark 6.1–6 *or,* 1st EP of Peter and Paul, Apostles [*or* †Peter the Apostle alone]: Psalms 66, 67; Ezekiel 3.4–11; Galatians 1.13—2.8 [†Acts 9.32–end]
Monday	**30 June** *R* Peter and Paul, Apostles *(transferred from Sunday 29 June)* *or* *R* Peter the Apostle *(transferred from Sunday 29 June)*	*Peter and Paul:* Zechariah 4.1–6*a*, 10*b*–end *or* Acts 12.1–11 Psalm 125 Acts 12.1–11 *or* 2 Timothy 4.6–8, 17–18 Matthew 16.13–19	*Peter alone:* Ezekiel 3.22–end *or* Acts 12.1–11 Psalm 125 Acts 12.1–11 *or* 1 Peter 2.19–end Matthew 16.13–19	*MP* Psalms 71, 113 Isaiah 49.1–6 Acts 11.1–18	*EP* Psalms 124, 138 Ezekiel 34.11–16 John 21.15–22

Trinity 2

Day	Date	Colour	Holy Communion	Morning Prayer	Evening Prayer
Tuesday	**1 July** *Henry, John, and Henry Venn, priests, evangelical divines, 1797, 1813, 1873* DEL week 13	*G*	Genesis 19.15–29 Psalm 26 Matthew 8.23–27	Psalms **48**, 52 Job 21 Romans 9.19–end	Psalm **50** Judges 4.1–23 Luke 13.10–21
Wednesday	**2 July**	*G*	Genesis 21.5, 8–20 Psalm 34.1–12 Matthew 8.28–end	Psalm **119.57–80** Job 22 Romans 10.1–10	Psalms **59**, 60 (67) Judges 5 Luke 13.22–end *or:* 1st EP of Thomas the Apostle: Psalm 27; Isaiah 35; Hebrews 10.35—11.1

Day	Date	Colour	Principal Service	3rd Service	2nd Service
Thursday	**3 July** Thomas the Apostle	*R*	Habakkuk 2.1–4 Psalm 31.1–6 Ephesians 2.19–end John 20.24–29	*MP* Psalms 92, 146 2 Samuel 15.17–21 *or* Ecclesiasticus 2 John 11.1–16	*EP* Psalm 139 Job 42.1–6 1 Peter 1.3–12

Day	Date	Colour	Holy Communion	Morning Prayer	Evening Prayer
Friday	**4 July**	*G*	Genesis 23.1–4, 19, 24.1–8, 62–end Psalm 106.1–5 Matthew 9.9–13	Psalms **51**, 54 Job 24 Romans 11.1–12	Psalm **38** Judges 6.25–end Luke 14.12–24
Saturday	**5 July**	*G*	Genesis 27.1–5*a*, 15–29 Psalm 135.1–6 Matthew 9.14–17	Psalm **68** Job 25—26 Romans 11.13–24	Psalms 65, **66** Judges 7 Luke 14.25–end

			Principal Service	3rd Service	2nd Service
Sunday	**6 July** **3rd Sunday after Trinity** Proper 9	*G*	*Continuous:* 2 Kings 5.1–14; Psalm 30 *Related:* Isaiah 66.10–14; Psalm 66.1–8 Galatians 6. [1–6] 7–16 Luke 10.1–11, 16–20	Psalm 74 Deuteronomy 24.10–end Acts 28.1–16	Psalms 65 [70] Genesis 29.1–20 Mark 6.7–29
			Holy Communion	**Morning Prayer**	**Evening Prayer**
Monday	**7 July** DEL week 14	*G*	Genesis 28.10–end Psalm 91.1–10 Matthew 9.18–26	Psalm **71** Job 27 Romans 11.25–end	Psalms **72**, 75 Judges 8.22–end Luke 15.1–10
Tuesday	**8 July**	*G*	Genesis 32.22–end Psalm 17.1–8 Matthew 9.32–end	Psalm **73** Job 28 Romans 12.1–8	Psalm **74** Judges 9.1–21 Luke 15.11–end
Wednesday	**9 July**	*G*	Genesis 41.55–end, 42.5–7, 17–end Psalm 33.1–4, 18–end Matthew 10.1–7	Psalm **77** Job 29 Romans 12.9–end	Psalm **119.81–104** Judges 9.22–end Luke 16.1–18
Thursday	**10 July**	*G*	Genesis 44.18–21, 23–29, 45.1–5 Psalm 105.11–17 Matthew 10.7–15	Psalm **78.1–39*** Job 30 Romans 13.1–7	Psalm **78.40–end*** Judges 11.1–11 Luke 16.19–end
Friday	**11 July** Benedict, abbot, c.550 (see p.82)	*Gw*	Genesis 46.1–7, 28–30 Psalm 37.3–6, 27–28 Matthew 10.16–23	Psalm **55** Job 31 Romans 13.8–end	Psalm **69** Judges 11.29–end Luke 17.1–10
Saturday	**12 July**	*G*	Genesis 49.29–end, 50.15–24 Psalm 105.1–7 Matthew 10.24–33	Psalms **76**, 79 Job 32 Romans 14.1–12	Psalms 81, **84** Judges 12.1–7 Luke 17.11–19

Trinity 4

Day	Date	Colour	Principal Service	3rd Service	2nd Service
Sunday	**13 July** **4th Sunday after Trinity** Proper 10	*G*	*Continuous:* Amos 7.7–end Psalm 82 *Related:* Deuteronomy 30.9–14 Psalm 25.1–10 Colossians 1.1–14 Luke 10.25–37	Psalm 76 Deuteronomy 28.1–14 Acts 28.17–end	Psalm 77 [*or* 77.1–12] Genesis 32.9–30 Mark 7.1–23
			Holy Communion	**Morning Prayer**	**Evening Prayer**
Monday	**14 July** John Keble, priest, poet, 1866 (see p.81) DEL week 15	*Gw*	Exodus 1.8–14, 22 Psalm 124 Matthew 10.34—11.1	Psalms **80**, 82 Job 33 Romans 14.13–end	Psalms **85**, 86 Judges 13.1–24 Luke 17.20–end
Tuesday	**15 July** Swithun, bishop, c.862 (see p.81) *Bonaventure, friar, bishop, teacher of the faith, 1274*	*Gw*	Exodus 2.1–15 Psalm 69.1–2, 31–end Matthew 11.20–24	Psalms 87, **89.1–18** Job 38 Romans 15.1–13	Psalm **89.19–end** Judges 14 Luke 18.1–14
Wednesday	**16 July** *Osmund, bishop, 1099*	*G*	Exodus 3.1–6, 9–12 Psalm 103.1–7 Matthew 11.25–27	Psalm **119.105–128** Job 39 Romans 15.14–21	Psalms **91**, 93 Judges 15.1—16.3 Luke 18.15–30
Thursday	**17 July**	*G*	Exodus 3.13–20 Psalm 105.1–2, 23 Matthew 11.28–end	Psalms 90, **92** Job 40 Romans 15.22–end	Psalm **94** Judges 16.4–end Luke 18.31–end
Friday	**18 July** *Elizabeth Ferard, deaconess, founder of the Community of St Andrew, 1883*	*G*	Exodus 11.10—12.14 Psalm 116.10–end Matthew 12.1–8	Psalms **88** (95) Job 41 Romans 16.1–16	Psalm **102** Judges 17 Luke 19.1–10
Saturday	**19 July** Gregory, bishop, and his sister Macrina, deaconess, teachers of the faith, c.394 and c.379 (see p.80)	*Gw*	Exodus 12.37–42 Psalm 136.1–4, 10–15 Matthew 12.14–21	Psalms 96, **97**, 100 Job 42 Romans 16.17–end	Psalm **104** Judges 18.1–20, 27–end Luke 19.11–27

Trinity 5

Day	Date	Colour	Service	Service	Service
			Principal Service	**3rd Service**	**2nd Service**
Sunday	**20 July** **5th Sunday after Trinity** Proper 11	*G*	*Continuous:* Amos 8.1–12 Psalm 52 *Related:* Genesis 18.1–10*a* Psalm 15 Colossians 1.15–28 Luke 10.38–end	Psalms 82, 100 Deuteronomy 30.1–10 1 Peter 3.8–18	Psalm 81 Genesis 41.1–16, 25–37 1 Corinthians 4.8–13 *HC* John 4.31–35
			Holy Communion	**Morning Prayer**	**Evening Prayer**
Monday	**21 July** DEL week 16	*G*	Exodus 14.5–18 Psalm 136.1–4, 10–15 *or Canticle:* Exodus 15.1–6 Matthew 12.38–42	Psalms **98**, 99, 101 Ezekiel 1.1–14 2 Corinthians 1.1–14	Psalm **105*** (*or* 103) 1 Samuel 1.1–20 Luke 19.28–40
				or: 1st EP of Mary Magdalene: Psalm 139; Isaiah 25.1–9; 2 Corinthians 1.3–7	
			Principal Service	**3rd Service**	**2nd Service**
Tuesday	**22 July** Mary Magdalene	*W*	Song of Solomon 3.1–4 Psalm 42.1–10 2 Corinthians 5.14–17 John 20.1–2, 11–18	*MP* Psalms 30, 32, 150 1 Samuel 16.14–end Luke 8.1–3	*EP* Psalm 63 Zephaniah 3.14–end Mark 15.40—16.7
			Holy Communion	**Morning Prayer**	**Evening Prayer**
Wednesday	**23 July** *Bridget, abbess, 1373*	*G*	Exodus 16.1–5, 9–15 Psalm 78.17–31 Matthew 13.1–9	Psalms 110, **111**, 112 Ezekiel 2.3—3.11 2 Corinthians 2.5–end	Psalm **119.129–152** 1 Samuel 2.12–26 Luke 20.1–8
Thursday	**24 July**	*G*	Exodus 19.1–2, 9–11, 16–20 *Canticle:* Bless the Lord Matthew 13.10–17	Psalms 113, **115** Ezekiel 3.12–end 2 Corinthians 3	Psalms 114, **116**, 117 1 Samuel 2.27–end Luke 20.9–19
				or: 1st EP of James the Apostle: Psalm 144; Deuteronomy 30.11–end; Mark 5.21–end	
			Principal Service	**3rd Service**	**2nd Service**
Friday	**25 July** James the Apostle	*R*	Jeremiah 45.1–5 *or* Acts 11.27—12.2 Psalm 126 Acts 11.27—12.2 *or* 2 Corinthians 4.7–15 Matthew 20.20–28	*MP* Psalms 7, 29, 117 2 Kings 1.9–15 Luke 9.46–56	*EP* Psalm 94 Jeremiah 26.1–15 Mark 1.14–20
			Holy Communion	**Morning Prayer**	**Evening Prayer**
Saturday	**26 July** Anne and Joachim, parents of the Blessed Virgin Mary	*Gw*	Exodus 24.3–8 Psalm 50.1–6, 14–15 Matthew 13.24–30 *Lesser Festival eucharistic lectionary:* Zephaniah 3.14–18*a*; Psalm 127; Romans 8.28–30; Matthew 13.16–17	Psalms 120, **121**, 122 Ezekiel 9 2 Corinthians 5	Psalm **118** 1 Samuel 4.1*b*–end Luke 20.27–40

Trinity 6

Day	Date		Principal Service	3rd Service	2nd Service
Sunday	**27 July** **6th Sunday after Trinity** Proper 12	*G*	*Continuous:* Hosea 1.2–10 Psalm 85 [*or* 85.1–7] *Related:* Genesis 18.20–32 Psalm 138 Colossians 2.6–15 [16–19] Luke 11.1–13	Psalm 95 Song of Solomon 2 *or* 1 Maccabees 2. [1–14] 15–22 1 Peter 4.7–14	Psalm 88 [*or* 88.1–10] Genesis 42.1–25 1 Corinthians 10.1–24 *HC* Matthew 13.24–30 [31–43]
			Holy Communion	**Morning Prayer**	**Evening Prayer**
Monday	**28 July** DEL week 17	*G*	Exodus 32.15–24, 30–34 Psalm 106.19–23 Matthew 13.31–35	Psalms 123, 124, 125, **126** Ezekiel 10.1–19 2 Corinthians 6.1—7.1	Psalms **127**, 128, 129 1 Samuel 5 Luke 20.41—21.4
Tuesday	**29 July** Mary, Martha and Lazarus, companions of Our Lord	*Gw*	Exodus 33.7–11; 34.5–9, 28 Psalm 103.8–12 Matthew 13.36–43 *Lesser Festival eucharistic lectionary:* Isaiah 25.6–9 Psalm 49.5–10, 16 Hebrews 2.10–15 John 12.1–8	Psalms **132**, 133 Ezekiel 11.14–end 2 Corinthians 7.2–end	Psalms (134,) **135** 1 Samuel 6.1–16 Luke 21.5–19
Wednesday	**30 July** William Wilberforce, social reformer, Olaudah Equiano and Thomas Clarkson anti-slavery campaigners, 1833, 1797 and 1846 (see p.83)	*Gw*	Exodus 34.29–end Psalm 99 Matthew 13.44–46	Psalm **119.153–end** Ezekiel 12.1–16 2 Corinthians 8.1–15	Psalm **136** 1 Samuel 7 Luke 21.20–28
Thursday	**31 July** *Ignatius of Loyola, founder of the Society of Jesus, 1556*	*G*	Exodus 40.16–21, 34–end Psalm 84.1–6 Matthew 13.47–53	Psalms **143**, 146 Ezekiel 12.17–end 2 Corinthians 8.16—9.5	Psalms **138**, 140, 141 1 Samuel 8 Luke 21.29–end
Friday	**1 August**	*G*	Leviticus 23.1, 4–11, 15–16, 27, 34–37 Psalm 81.1–8 Matthew 13.54–end	Psalms 142, **144** Ezekiel 13.1–16 2 Corinthians 9.6–end	Psalm **145** 1 Samuel 9.1–14 Luke 22.1–13
Saturday	**2 August**	*G*	Leviticus 25.1, 8–17 Psalm 67 Matthew 14.1–12	Psalm **147** Ezekiel 14.1–11 2 Corinthians 10	Psalms **148**, 149, 150 1 Samuel 9.15—10.1 Luke 22.14–23

Day	Date	Principal Service		3rd Service	2nd Service
		Continuous:	*Related:*		
Sunday	**3 August** *G* **7th Sunday after Trinity** Proper 13	Hosea 11.1–11 Psalm 107.1–9, 43 [*or* 107.1–9]	Ecclesiastes 1.2, 12–14; 2.18–23 Psalm 49.1–12 [*or* 49.1–9]	Psalm 106.1–10 Song of Solomon 5.2–end *or* 1 Maccabees 3.1–12 2 Peter 1.1–15	Psalm 107.1–32 [*or* 107.1–12] Genesis 50.4–end 1 Corinthians 14.1–19 *HC* Mark 6.45–52
		Colossians 3.1–11 Luke 12.13–21			

Day	Date	Holy Communion	Morning Prayer	Evening Prayer
Monday	**4 August** *G* *Jean-Baptiste Vianney, curé d'Ars, spiritual guide, 1859* DEL week 18	Numbers 11.4–15 Psalm 81.11–end Matthew 14.13–21 *or* 14.22–end	Psalms **1**, 2, 3 Ezekiel 14.12–end 2 Corinthians 11.1–15	Psalms **4**, 7 1 Samuel 10.1–16 Luke 22.24–30
Tuesday	**5 August** *Gr* Oswald, king, martyr, 642 (see p.79)	Numbers 12.1–13 Psalm 51.1–8 Matthew 14.22–end *or* 15.1–2, 10–14	Psalms **5**, 6 (8) Ezekiel 18.1–20 2 Corinthians 11.16–end	Psalms **9**, 10* 1 Samuel 10.17–end Luke 22.31–38 *or:* 1st EP of the Transfiguration of Our Lord: Psalms 99, 110; Exodus 24.12–end; John 12.27–36*a*

Day	Date	Principal Service	3rd Service	2nd Service
Wednesday	**6 August** *Gold or W* Transfiguration of Our Lord	Daniel 7.9–10, 13–14 Psalm 97 2 Peter 1.16–19 Luke 9.28–36	*MP* Psalms 27, 150 Ecclesiasticus 48.1–10 *or* 1 Kings 19.1–16 1 John 3.1–3	*EP* Psalm 72 Exodus 34.29–end 2 Corinthians 3

Day	Date	Holy Communion	Morning Prayer	Evening Prayer
Thursday	**7 August** *G* *John Mason Neale, priest, hymn writer, 1866*	Numbers 20.1–13 Psalm 95.1, 8–end Matthew 16.13–23	Psalms 14, **15**, 16 Ezekiel 20.1–20 2 Corinthians 13	Psalm **18*** 1 Samuel 12 Luke 22.47–62
Friday	**8 August** *Gw* Dominic, priest, founder of the Order of Preachers, 1221 (see p.82)	Deuteronomy 4.32–40 Psalm 77.11–end Matthew 16.24–end	Psalms 17, **19** Ezekiel 20.21–38 James 1.1–11	Psalm **22** 1 Samuel 13.5–18 Luke 22.63–end
Saturday	**9 August** *Gw* Mary Sumner, founder of the Mothers' Union, 1921 (see p.83)	Deuteronomy 6.4–13 Psalm 18.1–2, 48–end Matthew 17.14–20	Psalms 20, 21, **23** Ezekiel 24.15–end James 1.12–end	Psalms **24**, 25 1 Samuel 13.19—14.15 Luke 23.1–12

Trinity 8

		Principal Service	3rd Service	2nd Service
Sunday	**10 August** *G* **8th Sunday after Trinity** Proper 14	*Continuous:* Isaiah 1.1, 10–20 Psalm 50.1–8, 23–end [*or* 50.1–7] *Related:* Genesis 15.1–6 Psalm 33.12–end [*or* 33.12–21] Hebrews 11.1–3, 8–16 Luke 12.32–40	Psalm 115 Song of Solomon 8.5–7 *or* 1 Maccabees 14.4–15 2 Peter 3.8–13	Psalms 108 [116] Isaiah 11.10—end of 12 2 Corinthians 1.1–22 *HC* Mark 7.24–30
		Holy Communion	**Morning Prayer**	**Evening Prayer**
Monday	**11 August** *Gw* Clare of Assisi, founder of the Poor Clares, 1253 (see p.82) *John Henry Newman, priest, 1890* DEL week 19	Deuteronomy 10.12–end Psalm 147.13–end Matthew 17.22–end	Psalms 27, **30** Ezekiel 28.1–19 James 2.1–13	Psalms 26, **28**, 29 1 Samuel 14.24–46 Luke 23.13–25
Tuesday	**12 August** *G*	Deuteronomy 31.1–8 Psalm 107.1–3, 42–end *or Canticle:* Deuteronomy 32.3–4, 7–9 Matthew 18.1–5, 10, 12–14	Psalms 32, **36** Ezekiel 33.1–20 James 2.14–end	Psalm **33** 1 Samuel 15.1–23 Luke 23.26–43
Wednesday	**13 August** *Gw* Jeremy Taylor, bishop, teacher of the faith, 1667 (see p.80) *Florence Nightingale, nurse, social reformer, 1910* *Octavia Hill, social reformer, 1912*	Deuteronomy 34 Psalm 66.14–end Matthew 18.15–20	Psalm **34** Ezekiel 33.21–end James 3	Psalm **119.33–56** 1 Samuel 16 Luke 23.44–56*a*
Thursday	**14 August** *G* *Maximilian Kolbe, friar, martyr, 1941*	Joshua 3.7–11, 13–17 Psalm 114 Matthew 18.21—19.1	Psalm **37*** Ezekiel 34.1–16 James 4.1–12	Psalms 39, **40** 1 Samuel 17.1–30 Luke 23.56*b*—24.12
			or: 1st EP of the Blessed Virgin Mary: Psalm 72; Proverbs 8.22–31; John 19.23–27	
		Principal Service	**3rd Service**	**2nd Service**
Friday	**15 August** *W* The Blessed Virgin Mary	Isaiah 61.10–end *or* Revelation 11.19—12.6, 10 Psalm 45.10–end Galatians 4.4–7 Luke 1.46–55	*MP* Psalms 98, 138, 147.1–12 Isaiah 7.10–15 Luke 11.27–28	*EP* Psalm 132 Song of Solomon 2.1–7 Acts 1.6–14
		Holy Communion	**Morning Prayer**	**Evening Prayer**
Saturday	**16 August** *G*	Joshua 24.14–29 Psalm 16.1, 5–end Matthew 19.13–15	Psalms 41, **42**, 43 Ezekiel 36.16–36 James 5.7–end	Psalms 45, **46** 1 Samuel 17.55—18.6 Luke 24.36–end

Day	Date		Principal Service		3rd Service	2nd Service
Sunday	**17 August** **9th Sunday after Trinity** Proper 15	*G*	*Continuous:* Isaiah 5.1–7 Psalm 80.1–2, 9–end [*or* 80.9–end] Hebrews 11.29—12.2 Luke 12.49–56	*Related:* Jeremiah 23.23–29 Psalm 82	Psalm 119.33–48 Jonah 1 *or* Ecclesiasticus 3.1–15 2 Peter 3.14–end	Psalm 119.17–32 [*or* 119.17–24] Isaiah 28.9–22 2 Corinthians 8.1–9 *HC* Matthew 20.1–16
			Holy Communion		**Morning Prayer**	**Evening Prayer**
Monday	**18 August** DEL week 20	*G*	Judges 2.11–19 Psalm 106.34–42 Matthew 19.16–22		Psalm **44** Ezekiel 37.1–14 Mark 1.1–13	Psalms **47**, 49 1 Samuel 19.1–18 Acts 1.1–14
Tuesday	**19 August**	*G*	Judges 6.11–24 Psalm 85.8–end Matthew 19.23–end		Psalms **48**, 52 Ezekiel 37.15–end Mark 1.14–20	Psalm **50** 1 Samuel 20.1–17 Acts 1.15–end
Wednesday	**20 August** Bernard, abbot, teacher of the faith, 1153 (see p.80) *William and Catherine Booth, founders of the Salvation Army, 1912, 1890*	*Gw*	Judges 9.6–15 Psalm 21.1–6 Matthew 20.1–16		Psalm **119.57–80** Ezekiel 39.21–end Mark 1.21–28	Psalms **59**, 60 (67) 1 Samuel 20.18–end Acts 2.1–21
Thursday	**21 August**	*G*	Judges 11.29–end Psalm 40.4–11 Matthew 22.1–14		Psalms 56, **57** (63*) Ezekiel 43.1–12 Mark 1.29–end	Psalms 61, **62**, 64 1 Samuel 21.1—22.5 Acts 2.22–36
Friday	**22 August**	*G*	Ruth 1.1, 3–6, 14–16, 22 Psalm 146 Matthew 22.34–40		Psalms **51**, 54 Ezekiel 44.4–16 Mark 2.1–12	Psalm **38** 1 Samuel 22.6–end Acts 2.37–end
Saturday	**23 August**	*G*	Ruth 2.1–3, 8–11, 4.13–17 Psalm 128 Matthew 23.1–12		Psalm **68** Ezekiel 47.1–12 Mark 2.13–22	Psalms 65, **66** 1 Samuel 23 Acts 3.1–10

or, if Bartholomew the Apostle *is celebrated on 24 August:*
1st EP of Bartholomew the Apostle:
Psalm 97; Isaiah 61.1–9;
2 Corinthians 6.1–10

Bartholomew / Trinity 10

If Bartholomew the Apostle is celebrated on Sunday 24 August:

		Principal Service	3rd Service	2nd Service
Sunday	**24 August** *R* Bartholomew the Apostle	Isaiah 43.8–13 *or* Acts 5.12–16 Psalm 145.1–7 Acts 5.12–16 *or* 1 Corinthians 4.9–15 Luke 22.24–30	*MP* Psalms 86, 117 Genesis 28.10–17 John 1.43–end	*EP* Psalms 91, 116 Ecclesiasticus 39.1–10 *or* Deuteronomy 18.15–19 Matthew 10.1–22
		Holy Communion	**Morning Prayer**	**Evening Prayer**
Monday	**25 August** *G* DEL week 21	1 Thessalonians 1.1–5, 8–end Psalm 149.1–5 Matthew 23.13–22	Psalm **71** Proverbs 1.1–19 Mark 2.23—3.6	Psalms **72**, 75 1 Samuel 24 Acts 3.11–end

If Bartholomew the Apostle is transferred to Monday 25 August:

		Principal Service	3rd Service	2nd Service
Sunday	**24 August** *G* **10th Sunday after Trinity** Proper 16	*Continuous:* Jeremiah 1.4–10 Psalm 71.1–6 *Related:* Isaiah 58.9*b*–end Psalm 103.1–8 Hebrews 12.18–end Luke 13.10–17	Psalm 119.73–88 Jonah 2 *or* Ecclesiasticus 3.17–29 Revelation 1	Psalm 119.49–72 [*or* 119.49–56] Isaiah 30.8–21 2 Corinthians 9 *HC* Matthew 21.28–32 *or:* 1st EP of Bartholomew the Apostle: Psalm 97; Isaiah 61.1–9; 2 Corinthians 6.1–10
Monday	**25 August** *R* Bartholomew the Apostle *(transferred from Sunday 24 August)*	Isaiah 43.8–13 *or* Acts 5.12–16 Psalm 145.1–7 Acts 5.12–16 *or* 1 Corinthians 4.9–15 Luke 22.24–30	*MP* Psalms 86, 117 Genesis 28.10–17 John 1.43–end	*EP* Psalms 91, 116 Ecclesiasticus 39.1–10 *or* Deuteronomy 18.15–19 Matthew 10.1–22

			Holy Communion	Morning Prayer	Evening Prayer
Tuesday	**26 August** DEL week 21	*G*	I Thessalonians 2.1–8 Psalm 139.1–9 Matthew 23.23–26	Psalm **73** Proverbs 1.20–end Mark 3.7–19*a*	Psalm **74** I Samuel 26 Acts 4.1–12
Wednesday	**27 August** Monica, mother of Augustine of Hippo, 387 (see p.83)	*Gw*	I Thessalonians 2.9–13 Psalm 126 Matthew 23.27–32	Psalm **77** Proverbs 2 Mark 3.19*b*–end	Psalm **119.81–104** I Samuel 28.3–end Acts 4.13–31
Thursday	**28 August** Augustine, bishop, teacher of the faith, 430 (see p.80)	*Gw*	I Thessalonians 3.7–end Psalm 90.13–end Matthew 24.42–end	Psalm **78.1–39*** Proverbs 3.1–26 Mark 4.1–20	Psalm **78.40–end*** I Samuel 31 Acts 4.32—5.11
Friday	**29 August** Beheading of John the Baptist	*Gr*	I Thessalonians 4.1–8 Psalm 97 Matthew 25.1–13 *Lesser Festival eucharistic lectionary:* Jeremiah 1.4–10 Psalm 11 Hebrews 11.32—12.2 Matthew 14.1–12	Psalm **55** Proverbs 3.27—4.19 Mark 4.21–34	Psalm **69** 2 Samuel 1 Acts 5.12–26
Saturday	**30 August** John Bunyan, spiritual writer, 1688 (see p.80)	*Gw*	I Thessalonians 4.9–12 Psalm 98.1–2, 8–end Matthew 25.14–30	Psalms **76**, 79 Proverbs 6.1–19 Mark 4.35–end	Psalms 81, **84** 2 Samuel 2.1–11 Acts 5.27–end

Trinity 11

			Principal Service		3rd Service	2nd Service
Sunday	**31 August** **11th Sunday after Trinity** Proper 17	*G*	*Continuous:* Jeremiah 2.4–13 Psalm 81.1, 10–end [*or* 81.1–11] Hebrews 13.1–8, 15–16 Luke 14.1, 7–14	*Related:* Ecclesiasticus 10.12–18 *or* Proverbs 25.6–7 Psalm 112	Psalm 119.161–end Jonah 3.1–9 *or* Ecclesiasticus 11.[7–17] 18–28 Revelation 3.14–22	Psalm 119.81–96 [*or* 119.81–88] Isaiah 33.13–22 John 3.22–36

			Holy Communion	Morning Prayer	Evening Prayer
Monday	**1 September** *Giles, hermit, c.710* DEL week 22	*G*	1 Thessalonians 4.13–end Psalm 96 Luke 4.16–30	Psalms **80**, 82 Proverbs 8.1–21 Mark 5.1–20	Psalms **85**, 86 2 Samuel 3.12–end Acts 6
Tuesday	**2 September** *Martyrs of Papua New Guinea, 1901, 1942*	*G*	1 Thessalonians 5.1–6, 9–11 Psalm 27.1–8 Luke 4.31–37	Psalms 87, **89.1–18** Proverbs 8.22–end Mark 5.21–34	Psalm **89.19–end** 2 Samuel 5.1–12 Acts 7.1–16
Wednesday	**3 September** Gregory the Great, bishop, teacher of the faith, 604 (see p.80)	*Gw*	Colossians 1.1–8 Psalm 34.11–18 Luke 4.38–end	Psalm **119.105–128** Proverbs 9 Mark 5.35–end	Psalms **91**, 93 2 Samuel 6.1–19 Acts 7.17–43
Thursday	**4 September** *Birinus, bishop, 650*	*G*	Colossians 1.9–14 Psalm 98.1–5 Luke 5.1–11	Psalms 90, **92** Proverbs 10.1–12 Mark 6.1–13	Psalm **94** 2 Samuel 7.1–17 Acts 7.44–53
Friday	**5 September**	*G*	Colossians 1.15–20 Psalm 89.19*b*–28 Luke 5.33–end	Psalms **88** (95) Proverbs 11.1–12 Mark 6.14–29	Psalm **102** 2 Samuel 7.18–end Acts 7.54—8.3
Saturday	**6 September** *Allen Gardiner, missionary, founder of the South American Mission Society, 1851*	*G*	Colossians 1.21–23 Psalm 117 Luke 6.1–5	Psalms 96, **97**, 100 Proverbs 12.10–end Mark 6.30–44	Psalm **104** 2 Samuel 9 Acts 8.4–25

Trinity 12

		Principal Service	3rd Service	2nd Service
Sunday	**7 September** *G* **12th Sunday after Trinity** Proper 18	*Continuous:* Jeremiah 18.1–11 Psalm 139.1–5, 12–18 [*or* 139.1–7] *Related:* Deuteronomy 30.15–end Psalm 1 Philemon 1–21 Luke 14.25–33	Psalms 122, 123 Jonah 3.10—end of 4 *or* Ecclesiasticus 27.30—28.9 Revelation 8.1–5	Psalms [120] 121 Isaiah 43.14—44.5 John 5.30–end
		Holy Communion	**Morning Prayer**	**Evening Prayer**
Monday	**8 September** *Gw* Birth of the Blessed Virgin Mary (see p.79) *Accession of King Charles III, 2022 (see p.85)* DEL week 23	Colossians 1.24—2.3 Psalm 62.1–7 Luke 6.6–11	Psalms **98**, 99, 101 Proverbs 14.31—15.17 Mark 6.45–end	Psalm **105*** (*or* 103) 2 Samuel 11 Acts 8.26–end
	If the Festival of the Blessed Virgin Mary is transferred to 8 September, the provision (including 1st EP) for 15 August is used.			
Tuesday	**9 September** *G* *Charles Fuge Lowder, priest, 1880*	Colossians 2.6–15 Psalm 8 Luke 6.12–19	Psalm **106*** (*or* 103) Proverbs 15.18–end Mark 7.1–13	Psalm **107*** 2 Samuel 12.1–25 Acts 9.1–19*a*
Wednesday	**10 September** *G*	Colossians 3.1–11 Psalm 15 Luke 6.20–26	Psalms 110, **111**, 112 Proverbs 18.10–end Mark 7.14–23	Psalm **119.129–152** 2 Samuel 15.1–12 Acts 9.19*b*–31
Thursday	**11 September** *G*	Colossians 3.12–17 Psalm 149.1–5 Luke 6.27–38	Psalms 113, **115** Proverbs 20.1–22 Mark 7.24–30	Psalms 114, **116**, 117 2 Samuel 15.13–end Acts 9.32–end
Friday	**12 September** *G*	1 Timothy 1.1–2, 12–14 Psalm 16 Luke 6.39–42	Psalm **139** Proverbs 22.1–16 Mark 7.31–end	Psalms **130**, 131, 137 2 Samuel 16.1–14 Acts 10.1–16
Saturday	**13 September** *Gw* John Chrysostom, bishop, teacher of the faith, 407 (see p.80)	1 Timothy 1.15–17 Psalm 113 Luke 6.43–end	Psalms 120, **121**, 122 Proverbs 24.23–end Mark 8.1–10	Psalm **118** 2 Samuel 17.1–23 Acts 10.17–33 *or, if* Holy Cross Day *is celebrated on Sunday 14 September:* 1st EP of Holy Cross Day: Psalm 66; Isaiah 52.13—end of 53; Ephesians 2.11–end

Holy Cross Day / Trinity 13

If Holy Cross Day is celebrated on Sunday 14 September:

		Principal Service	3rd Service	2nd Service
Sunday	**14 September** *R* Holy Cross Day	Numbers 21.4–9 Psalm 22.23–28 Philippians 2.6–11 John 3.13–17	*MP* Psalms 2, 8, 146 Genesis 3.1–15 John 12.27–36*a*	*EP* Psalms 110, 150 Isaiah 63.1–16 1 Corinthians 1.18–25
		Holy Communion	**Morning Prayer**	**Evening Prayer**
Monday	**15 September** *Gr* Cyprian, bishop, martyr, 258 (see p.79) DEL week 24	1 Timothy 2.1–8 Psalm 28 Luke 7.1–10	Psalms 123, 124, 125, **126** Proverbs 25.1–14 Mark 8.11–21	Psalms **127**, 128, 129 2 Samuel 18.1–18 Acts 10.34–end

If Holy Cross Day is transferred to Monday 15 September:

		Principal Service	3rd Service	2nd Service
Sunday	**14 September** *G* **13th Sunday after Trinity** Proper 19	*Continuous:* Jeremiah 4.11–12, 22–28; Psalm 14 *Related:* Exodus 32.7–14; Psalm 51.1–11 1 Timothy 1.12–17 Luke 15.1–10	Psalms 126, 127 Isaiah 44.24—45.8 Revelation 12.1–12	Psalms 124, 125 Isaiah 60 John 6.51–69 *or:* 1st EP of Holy Cross Day: Psalm 66; Isaiah 52.13—end of 53; Ephesians 2.11–end
Monday	**15 September** *R* Holy Cross Day	Numbers 21.4–9 Psalm 22.23–28 Philippians 2.6–11 John 3.13–17	*MP* Psalms 2, 8, 146 Genesis 3.1–15 John 12.27–36*a*	*EP* Psalms 110, 150 Isaiah 63.1–16 1 Corinthians 1.18–25

		Holy Communion	Morning Prayer	Evening Prayer
Tuesday	**16 September** *Gw* Ninian, bishop, apostle of the Picts, c.432 (see p.82) *Edward Bouverie Pusey, priest, 1882* DEL week 24	I Timothy 3.1–13 Psalm 101 Luke 7.11–17	Psalms **132**, 133 Proverbs 25.15–end Mark 8.22–26	Psalms (134), **135** 2 Samuel 18.19–19.8*a* Acts 11.1–18
Wednesday	**17 September** *Gw* Hildegard, abbess, visionary, 1179 (see p.82)	I Timothy 3.14–end Psalm 111.1–5 Luke 7.31–35	Psalm **119.153–end** Proverbs 26.12–end Mark 8.27—9.1	Psalm **136** 2 Samuel 19.8*b*–23 Acts 11.19–end
Thursday	**18 September** *G*	I Timothy 4.12–end Psalm 111.6–end Luke 7.36–end	Psalms **143**, 146 Proverbs 27.1–22 Mark 9.2–13	Psalms **138**, 140, 141 2 Samuel 19.24–end Acts 12.1–17
Friday	**19 September** *G* *Theodore, archbishop, 690*	I Timothy 6.2*b*–12 Psalm 49.1–9 Luke 8.1–3	Psalms 142, **144** Proverbs 30.1–9, 24–31 Mark 9.14–29	Psalm **145** 2 Samuel 23.1–7 Acts 12.18–end
Saturday	**20 September** *Gr* John Coleridge Patteson, bishop, and companions, martyrs, 1871 (see p.79)	I Timothy 6.13–16 Psalm 100 Luke 8.4–15	Psalm **147** Proverbs 31.10–end Mark 9.30–37	Psalms **148**, 149, 150 2 Samuel 24 Acts 13.1–12 *or, if* Matthew, Apostle and Evangelist *is celebrated on Sunday 21 September:* 1st EP of Matthew, Apostle and Evangelist: Psalm 34; Isaiah 33.13–17; Matthew 6.19–end

Matthew / Trinity 14

If Matthew, Apostle and Evangelist is celebrated on Sunday 21 September:

		Principal Service	3rd Service	2nd Service
Sunday	**21 September** *R* Matthew, Apostle and Evangelist	Proverbs 3.13–18 Psalm 119.65–72 2 Corinthians 4.1–6 Matthew 9.9–13	*MP* Psalms 49, 117 1 Kings 19.15–end 2 Timothy 3.14–end	*EP* Psalm 119.33–40, 89–96 Ecclesiastes 5.4–12 Matthew 19.16–end
		Holy Communion	**Morning Prayer**	**Evening Prayer**
Monday	**22 September** *G* DEL week 25	Ezra 1.1–6 Psalm 126 Luke 8.16–18	Psalms **1**, 2, 3 Wisdom 1 *or* 1 Chronicles. 10.1—11.9 Mark 9.38–end	Psalms **4**, 7 1 Kings 1.5–31 Acts 13.13–43

If Matthew, Apostle and Evangelist is transferred to Monday 22 September:

		Principal Service	3rd Service	2nd Service
Sunday	**21 September** *G* **14th Sunday after Trinity** Proper 20	*Continuous:* Jeremiah 8.18—9.1 Psalm 79.1–9 *Related:* Amos 8.4–7 Psalm 113 1 Timothy 2.1–7 Luke 16.1–13	Psalms 130, 131 Isaiah 45.9–22 Revelation 14.1–5	Psalms [128] 129 Ezra 1 John 7.14–36 *or:* 1st EP of Matthew, Apostle and Evangelist: Psalm 34; Isaiah 33.13–17; Matthew 6.19–end
Monday	**22 September** *R* Matthew, Apostle and Evangelist *(transferred from Sunday 21 September)*	Proverbs 3.13–18 Psalm 119.65–72 2 Corinthians 4.1–6 Matthew 9.9–13	*MP* Psalms 49, 117 1 Kings 19.15–end 2 Timothy 3.14–end	*EP* Psalm 119.33–40, 89–96 Ecclesiastes 5.4–12 Matthew 19.16–end

			Holy Communion	Morning Prayer	Evening Prayer
Tuesday	**23 September** DEL week 25	*G*	Ezra 6.7–8, 12, 14–20 Psalm 124 Luke 8.19–21	Psalms **5**, 6 (8) Wisdom 2 *or* 1 Chronicles 13 Mark 10.1–16	Psalms **9**, 10* 1 Kings 1.32—2.4; 2.10–12 Acts 13.44—14.7
Wednesday	**24 September** Ember Day	*G*	Ezra 9.5–9 *Canticle:* Song of Tobit *or* Psalm 103.1–6 Luke 9.1–6	Psalm **119.1–32** Wisdom 3.1–9 *or* 1 Chronicles 15.1—16.3 Mark 10.17–31	Psalms **11**, 12, 13 1 Kings 3 Acts 14.8–end
Thursday	**25 September** Lancelot Andrewes, bishop, spiritual writer, 1626 (see p.81) *Sergei of Radonezh, monastic reformer, teacher of the faith, 1392*	*Gw*	Haggai 1.1–8 Psalm 149.1–5 Luke 9.7–9	Psalms 14, **15**, 16 Wisdom 4.7–end *or* 1 Chronicles 17 Mark 10.32–34	Psalm **18*** 1 Kings 4.29—5.12 Acts 15.1–21
Friday	**26 September** *Wilson Carlile, founder of the Church Army, 1942* Ember Day	*G*	Haggai 1.15*b*—2.9 Psalm 43 Luke 9.18–22	Psalms 17, **19** Wisdom 5.1–16 *or* 1 Chronicles 21.1—22.1 Mark 10.35–45	Psalm **22** 1 Kings 6.1, 11–28 Acts 15.22–35
Saturday	**27 September** Vincent de Paul, founder of the Lazarists, 1660 (see p.82) Ember Day	*Gw*	Zechariah 2.1–5, 10–11 Psalm 125 *or Canticle:* Jeremiah 31.10–13 Luke 9.43*b*–45	Psalms 20, 21, **23** Wisdom 5.17—6.11 *or* 1 Chronicles 22.2–end Mark 10.46–end	Psalms **24**, 25 1 Kings 8.1–30 Acts 15.36—16.5

Day	Date	Principal Service	3rd Service	2nd Service
Sunday	**28 September** *G* **15th Sunday after Trinity** Proper 21	*Continuous:* Jeremiah 32.1–3*a*, 6–15 Psalm 91.1–6, 14–end [*or* 91.11–end] *Related:* Amos 6.1*a*, 4–7 Psalm 146 1 Timothy 6.6–19 Luke 16.19–end	Psalm 132 Isaiah 48.12–end Luke 11.37–end	Psalms 134, 135 [*or* 135.1–14] Nehemiah 2 John 8.31–38, 48–end *or:* 1st EP of Michael and All Angels: Psalm 91; 2 Kings 6.8–17; Matthew 18.1–6, 10
Monday	**29 September** *W* Michael and All Angels	Genesis 28.10–17 *or* Revelation 12.7–12 Psalm 103.19–end Revelation 12.7–12 *or* Hebrews 1.5–end John 1.47–end	*MP* Psalms 34, 150 Tobit 12.6–end *or* Daniel 12.1–4 Acts 12.1–11	*EP* Psalms 138, 148 Daniel 10.4–end Revelation 5
		Holy Communion	**Morning Prayer**	**Evening Prayer**
Tuesday	**30 September** *G* *Jerome, translator, teacher of the faith, 420* DEL week 26	Zechariah 8.20–end Psalm 87 Luke 9.51–56	Psalms 32, **36** Wisdom 7.1–14 *or* 1 Chronicles 28.11–end Mark 11.12–26	Psalm **33** 1 Kings 8.63—9.9 Acts 16.25–end
Wednesday	**1 October** *G* *Remigius, bishop, 533* *Anthony Ashley Cooper (Earl of Shaftesbury), social reformer, 1885*	Nehemiah 2.1–8 Psalm 137.1–6 Luke 9.57–end	Psalm **34** Wisdom 7.15—8.4 *or* 1 Chronicles 29.1–9 Mark 11.27–end	Psalm **119.33–56** 1 Kings 10.1–25 Acts 17.1–15
Thursday	**2 October** *G*	Nehemiah 8.1–12 Psalm 19.7–11 Luke 10.1–12	Psalm **37*** Wisdom 8.5–18 *or* 1 Chronicles 29.10–20 Mark 12.1–12	Psalms 39, **40** 1 Kings 11.1–13 Acts 17.16–end
Friday	**3 October** *G* *George Bell, bishop, ecumenist, peacemaker, 1958*	Baruch 1.15–end *or* Deuteronomy 31.7–13 Psalm 79.1–9 Luke 10.13–16	Psalm **31** Wisdom 8.21—end of 9 *or* 1 Chronicles 29.21–end Mark 12.13–17	Psalm **35** 1 Kings 11.26–end Acts 18.1–21
Saturday	**4 October** *Gw* Francis of Assisi, friar, deacon, 1226 (see p.82)	Baruch 4.5–12, 27–29 *or* Joshua 22.1–6 Psalm 69.33–37 Luke 10.17–24	Psalms 41, **42**, 43 Wisdom 10.15—11.10 *or* 2 Chronicles 1.1–13 Mark 12.18–27	Psalms 45, **46** 1 Kings 12.1–24 Acts 18.22—19.7

		Principal Service	3rd Service	2nd Service
Sunday	**5 October** *G* **16th Sunday after Trinity** Proper 22	*Continuous:* Lamentations 1.1–6 *Canticle:* Lamentations 3.19–26 *or* Psalm 137 [*or* 137.1–6] *Related:* Habakkuk 1.1–4; 2.1–4 Psalm 37.1–9 2 Timothy 1.1–14 Luke 17.5–10	Psalm 141 Isaiah 49.13–23 Luke 12.1–12	Psalm 142 Nehemiah 5.1–13 John 9
		Holy Communion	**Morning Prayer**	**Evening Prayer**
Monday	**6 October** *Gr* William Tyndale, translator, martyr, 1536 (see p.79) DEL week 27	Jonah 1.1—2.2, 10 *Canticle:* Jonah 2.2–4, 7 *or* Psalm 69.1–6 Luke 10.25–37	Psalm **44** Wisdom 11.21—12.2 *or* 2 Chronicles 2.1–16 Mark 12.28–34	Psalms **47**, 49 1 Kings 12.25—13.10 Acts 19.8–20
Tuesday	**7 October** *G*	Jonah 3 Psalm 130 Luke 10.38–end	Psalms **48**, 52 Wisdom 12.12–21 *or* 2 Chronicles 3 Mark 12.35–end	Psalm **50** 1 Kings 13.11–end Acts 19.21–end
Wednesday	**8 October** *G*	Jonah 4 Psalm 86.1–9 Luke 11.1–4	Psalm **119.57–80** Wisdom 13.1–9 *or* 2 Chronicles 5 Mark 13.1–13	Psalms **59**, 60 (67) 1 Kings 17 Acts 20.1–16
Thursday	**9 October** *G* *Denys, bishop, and companions, martyrs, c.250* *Robert Grosseteste, bishop, philosopher, scientist, 1253*	Malachi 3.13—4.2*a* Psalm 1 Luke 11.5–13	Psalms 56, **57** (63*) Wisdom 16.15—17.1 *or* 2 Chronicles 6.1–21 Mark 13.14–23	Psalms 61, **62**, 64 1 Kings 18.1–20 Acts 20.17–end
Friday	**10 October** *Gw* Paulinus, bishop, missionary, 644 (see p.82) *Thomas Traherne, poet, spiritual writer, 1674*	Joel 1.13–15, 2.1–2 Psalm 9.1–7 Luke 11.15–26	Psalms **51**, 54 Wisdom 18.6–19 *or* 2 Chronicles 6.22–end Mark.13.24–31	Psalm **38** 1 Kings 18.21–end Acts 21.1–16
Saturday	**11 October** *G* *Ethelburga, abbess, 675* *James the Deacon, companion of Paulinus, 7th cent.*	Joel 3.12–end Psalm 97.1, 8–end Luke 11.27–28	Psalm **68** Wisdom 19 *or* 2 Chronicles 7 Mark 13.32–end	Psalms 65, **66** 1 Kings 19 Acts 21.17–36

Trinity 17

		Principal Service	3rd Service	2nd Service
Sunday	**12 October** *G* **17th Sunday after Trinity** Proper 23	*Continuous:* Jeremiah 29.1, 4–7 Psalm 66.1–11 *Related:* 2 Kings 5.1–3, 7–15*c* Psalm 111 2 Timothy 2.8–15 Luke 17.11–19	Psalm 143 Isaiah 50.4–10 Luke 13.22–30	Psalm 144 Nehemiah 6.1–16 John 15.12–end
		Holy Communion	**Morning Prayer**	**Evening Prayer**
Monday	**13 October** *Gw* Edward the Confessor, king, 1066 (see p.83) DEL week 28	Romans 1.1–7 Psalm 98 Luke 11.29–32	Psalm **71** 1 Maccabees 1.1–19 *or* 2 Chronicles 9.1–12 Mark 14.1–11	Psalms **72**, 75 1 Kings 21 Acts 21.37—22.21
Tuesday	**14 October** *G*	Romans 1.16–25 Psalm 19.1–4 Luke 11.37–41	Psalm **73** 1 Maccabees 1.20–40 *or* 2 Chronicles 10.1—11.4 Mark 14.12–25	Psalm **74** 1 Kings 22.1–28 Acts 22.22—23.11
Wednesday	**15 October** *Gw* Teresa of Avila, teacher of the faith, 1582 (see p.80)	Romans 2.1–11 Psalm 62.1–8 Luke 11.42–46	Psalm **77** 1 Maccabees 1.41–end *or* 2 Chronicles 12 Mark 14.26–42	Psalm **119.81–104** 1 Kings 22.29–45 Acts 23.12–end
Thursday	**16 October** *G* *Nicholas Ridley and Hugh Latimer, bishops, martyrs, 1555*	Romans 3.21–30 Psalm 130 Luke 11.47–end	Psalm **78.1–39*** 1 Maccabees 2.1–28 *or* 2 Chronicles 13.1—14.1 Mark 14.43–52	Psalm **78.40–end*** 2 Kings 1.2–17 Acts 24.1–23
Friday	**17 October** *Gr* Ignatius, bishop, martyr, c.107 (see p.79)	Romans 4.1–8 Psalm 32 Luke 12.1–7	Psalm **55** 1 Maccabees 2.29–48 *or* 2 Chronicles 14.2–end Mark 14.53–65	Psalm **69** 2 Kings 2.1–18 Acts 24.24—25.12 *or:* 1st EP of Luke the Evangelist: Psalm 33; Hosea 6.1–3; 2 Timothy 3.10–end
		Principal Service	**3rd Service**	**2nd Service**
Saturday	**18 October** *R* Luke the Evangelist	Isaiah 35.3–6 *or* Acts 16.6–12*a* Psalm 147.1–7 2 Timothy 4.5–17 Luke 10.1–9	*MP* Psalms 145, 146 Isaiah 55 Luke 1.1–4	*EP* Psalm 103 Ecclesiasticus 38.1–14 *or* Isaiah 61.1–6 Colossians 4.7–end

Day	Date	Colour	Principal Service		3rd Service	2nd Service
Sunday	**19 October** **18th Sunday after Trinity** Proper 24	*G*	*Continuous* Jeremiah 31.27–34 Psalm 119.97–104 2 Timothy 3.14—4.5 Luke 18.1–8	*Related:* Genesis 32.22–31 Psalm 121	Psalm 147 Isaiah 54.1–14 Luke 13.31–end	Psalms [146] 149 Nehemiah 8.9–end John 16.1–11
			Holy Communion		**Morning Prayer**	**Evening Prayer**
Monday	**20 October** DEL week 29	*G*	Romans 4.20–end *Canticle:* Benedictus 1–6 Luke 12.13–21		Psalms **80**, 82 1 Maccabees 3.1–26 *or* 2 Chronicles 17.1–12 Mark 15.1–15	Psalms **85**, 86 2 Kings 5 Acts 26.1–23
Tuesday	**21 October**	*G*	Romans 5.12, 15, 17–end Psalm 40.7–12 Luke 12.35–38		Psalms 87, **89.1–18** 1 Maccabees 3.27–41 *or* 2 Chronicles 18.1–27 Mark 15.16–32	Psalm **89.19–end** 2 Kings 6.1–23 Acts 26.24–end
Wednesday	**22 October**	*G*	Romans 6.12–18 Psalm 124 Luke 12.39–48		Psalm **119.105–128** 1 Maccabees 3.42–end *or* 2 Chronicles 18.28—end of 19 Mark 15.33–41	Psalms **91**, 93 2 Kings 9.1–16 Acts 27.1–26
Thursday	**23 October**	*G*	Romans 6.19–end Psalm 1 Luke 12.49–53		Psalms 90, **92** 1 Maccabees 4.1–25 *or* 2 Chronicles 20.1–23 Mark 15.42–end	Psalm **94** 2 Kings 9.17–end Acts 27.27–end
Friday	**24 October**	*G*	Romans 7.18–end Psalm 119.33–40 Luke 12.54–end		Psalms **88** (95) 1 Maccabees 4.26–35 *or* 2 Chronicles 22.10—end of 23 Mark 16.1–8	Psalm **102** 2 Kings 12.1–19 Acts 28.1–16
Saturday	**25 October** *Crispin and Crispinian, martyrs, c.287*	*G*	Romans 8.1–11 Psalm 24.1–6 Luke 13.1–9		Psalms 96, **97**, 100 1 Maccabees 4.36–end *or* 2 Chronicles 24.1–22 Mark 16.9–end	Psalm **104** 2 Kings 17.1–23 Acts 28.17–end

Last after Trinity

Day	Date		Principal Service	3rd Service	2nd Service
Sunday	**26 October** **Last Sunday after Trinity** Proper 25	*G*	*Continuous:* Joel 2.23–end Psalm 65 [*or* 65.1–7] *Related:* Ecclesiasticus 35.12–17 *or* Jeremiah 14.7–10, 19–end Psalm 84.1–7 2 Timothy 4.6–8, 16–18 Luke 18.9–14	Psalm 119.105–128 Isaiah 59.9–20 Luke 14.1–14	Psalm 119.1–16 Ecclesiastes 11, 12 2 Timothy 2.1–7 *HC* Matthew 22.34–end

or, if the date of dedication of a church is not known, the Dedication Festival (Gold or W) may be celebrated today or on 5 October, or on a suitable date chosen locally (see p.78)

Day	Date		Principal Service	3rd Service	2nd Service
Sunday	**26 October** **Bible Sunday**	*G*	Isaiah 45.22–end Psalm 119.129–136 Romans 15.1–6 Luke 4.16–24	Psalm 119.105–128 1 Kings 22.1–17 Romans 15.4–13 *or* Luke 14.1–14	Psalm 119.1–16 Jeremiah 36.9–end Romans 10.5–17 *HC* Matthew 22.34–40

Day	Date		Holy Communion	Morning Prayer	Evening Prayer
Monday	**27 October** DEL week 30	*G*	Romans 8.12–17 Psalm 68.1–6 Luke 13.10–17	Psalms **98**, 99, 101 1 Maccabees 6.1–17 *or* 2 Chronicles 26.1–21 John 13.1–11	Psalm **105*** (*or* 103) 2 Kings 17.24–end Philippians 1.1–11

or: 1st EP of Simon and Jude, Apostles: Psalms 124, 125, 126; Deuteronomy 32.1–4; John 14.15–26

Day	Date		Principal Service	3rd Service	2nd Service
Tuesday	**28 October** Simon and Jude, Apostles	*R*	Isaiah 28.14–16 Psalm 119.89–96 Ephesians 2.19–end John 15.17–end	*MP* Psalms 116, 117 Wisdom 5.1–16 *or* Isaiah 45.18–end Luke 6.12–16	*EP* Psalm 119.1–16 1 Maccabees 2.42–66 *or* Jeremiah 3.11–18 Jude 1–4, 17–end

Day	Date		Holy Communion	Morning Prayer	Evening Prayer
Wednesday	**29 October** James Hannington, bishop, martyr, 1885 (see p.79)	*Gr*	Romans 8.26–30 Psalm 13 Luke 13.22–30	Psalms 110, **111**, 112 1 Maccabees 7.1–20 *or* 2 Chronicles 29.1–19 John 13.21–30	Psalm **119.129–152** 2 Kings 18.13–end Philippians 2.1–13
Thursday	**30 October**	*G*	Romans 8.31–end Psalm 109.20–26, 29–30 Luke 13.31–end	Psalms 113, **115** 1 Maccabees 7.21–end *or* 2 Chronicles 29.20–end John 13.31–end	Psalms 114, **116**, 117 2 Kings 19.1–19 Philippians 2.14–end
Friday	**31 October** *Martin Luther, reformer, 1546*	*G*	Romans 9.1–5 Psalm 147.13–end Luke 14.1–6	Psalm **139** 1 Maccabees 9.1–22 *or* 2 Chronicles 30 John 14.1–14	Psalms **130**, 131, 137 2 Kings 19.20–36 Philippians 3.1—4.1

or, if All Saints' Day is celebrated on Saturday 1 November only:
1st EP of All Saints' Day: Psalms 1, 5; Ecclesiasticus 44.1–15 *or* Isaiah 40.27–end; Revelation 19.6–10

All Saints' Day / 4 before Advent

All Saints' Day is celebrated either on Saturday 1 November or Sunday 2 November; if the latter there may be a supplementary celebration on 1 November.

			Principal Service	**3rd Service**	**2nd Service**
Saturday	**1 November** **All Saints' Day**	*Gold or W*	Daniel 7.1–3, 15–18 Psalm 149 Ephesians 1.11–end Luke 6.20–31	*MP* Psalms 15, 84, 149 Isaiah 35. Luke 9.18–27	*EP* Psalms 148, 150 Isaiah 65.17–end Hebrews 11.32—12.2

If All Saints' Day is celebrated on Saturday 1 November in addition to Sunday 2 November:

Or **Saturday**	**1 November** **All Saints' Day**	*Gold or W*	Isaiah 56.3–8 *or* 2 Esdras 2.42–end Psalm 33.1–5 Hebrews 12.18–24 Matthew 5.1–12	*MP* Psalms 111, 112, 117 Wisdom 5.1–16 *or* Jeremiah 31.31–34 2 Corinthians 4.5–12	*EP* Psalm 145 Isaiah 66.20–23 Colossians 1.9–14

If All Saints' Day is celebrated on Sunday 2 November only:

			Holy Communion	**Morning Prayer**	**Evening Prayer**
Or **Saturday**	**1 November**	G	Romans 11.1–2, 11–12, 25–29 Psalm 94.14–19 Luke 14.1, 7–11	Psalms 120, **121**, 122 1 Maccabees 13.41–end, 14.4–15 *or* 2 Chronicles 32.1–22 John 14.15–end	Psalm **118** 2 Kings 20 Philippians 4.2–end

or, if All Saints' Day is celebrated on Sunday 2 November only:
1st EP of All Saints' Day
Psalms 1, 5; Ecclesiasticus 44.1–15 *or* Isaiah 40.27–end
Revelation 19.6–10

If All Saints' Day is celebrated on Saturday 1 November:

			Principal Service	**3rd Service**	**2nd Service**
Sunday	**2 November** **4th Sunday before Advent**	*R/G*	Isaiah 1.10–18 Psalm 32.1–8 2 Thessalonians 1 Luke 19.1–10	Psalm 87 Job 26 Colossians 1.9–14	Psalm 145 [*or* 145.1–9] Lamentations 3.22–33 John 11. [1–31] 32–44

If All Saints' Day is celebrated on Sunday 2 November only:

Or **Sunday**	**2 November** **All Saints' Day**	*Gold or W*	Daniel 7.1–3, 15–18 Psalm 149 Ephesians 1.11–end Luke 6.20–31	*MP* Psalms 15, 84, 149 Isaiah 35 Luke 9.18–27	*EP* Psalms 148, 150 Isaiah 65.17–end Hebrews 11.32—12.2

4 before Advent

		Holy Communion	Morning Prayer	Evening Prayer
Monday	**3 November** *Rw/Gw* Richard Hooker, priest, teacher of the faith, 1600 (see p.80) *Martin of Porres, friar, 1639* DEL week 31	Romans 11.29–end Psalm 69.31–37 Luke 14.12–14	Psalms **2**, 146 *or* 123, 124, 125, **126** Isaiah 1.1–20 Matthew 1.18–end	Psalms **92**, 96, 97 *or* **127**, 128, 129 Daniel 1 Revelation 1
Tuesday	**4 November** *R/G*	Romans 12.5–16 Psalm 131 Luke 14.15–24	Psalms **5**, 147.1–12 *or* **132**, 133 Isaiah 1.21–end Matthew 2.1–15	Psalms 98, 99, **100** *or* (134,) **135** Daniel 2.1–24 Revelation 2.1–11
Wednesday	**5 November** *R/G*	Romans 13.8–10 Psalm 112 Luke 14.25–33	Psalms **9**, 147.13–end *or* **119.153–end** Isaiah 2.1–11 Matthew 2.16–end	Psalms 111, **112**, 116 *or* **136** Daniel 2.25–end Revelation 2.12–end
Thursday	**6 November** *R/G* *Leonard, hermit, 6th cent.* *William Temple, archbishop,* *teacher of the faith, 1944*	Romans 14.7–12 Psalm 27.14–end Luke 15.1–10	Psalms 11, **15**, 148 *or* **143**, 146 Isaiah 2.12–end Matthew 3	Psalm **118** *or* **138**, 140, 141 Daniel 3.1–18 Revelation 3.1–13
Friday	**7 November** *Rw/Gw* Willibrord, bishop, 739 (see p.82)	Romans 15.14–21 Psalm 98 Luke 16.1–8	Psalms **16**, 149 *or* 142, **144** Isaiah 3.1–15 Matthew 4.1–11	Psalms 137, 138, **143** *or* **145** Daniel 3.19–end Revelation 3.14–end
Saturday	**8 November** *Rw/Gw* Saints and martyrs of England	Romans 16.3–9, 16, 22–end Psalm 145.1–7 Luke 16.9–15 *Lesser Festival eucharistic lectionary:* Isaiah 61.4–9 *or* Ecclesiasticus 44.1–15 Psalm 15 Revelation 19.5–10 John 17.18–23	Psalms **18.31–end**, 150 *or* **147** Isaiah 4.2—5.7 Matthew 4.12–22	Psalm **145** *or* **148**, 149, 150 Daniel 4.1–18 Revelation 4

		Principal Service	3rd Service	2nd Service
Sunday	**9 November** *R/G* **3rd Sunday before Advent** *Remembrance Sunday*	Job 19.23–27*a* Psalm 17.1–9 [*or* 17.1–8] 2 Thessalonians 2.1–5, 13–end Luke 20.27–38	Psalms 20, 90 Isaiah 2.1–5 James 3.13–end	Psalm 40 1 Kings 3.1–15 Romans 8.31–end *HC* Matthew 22.15–22
		Holy Communion	**Morning Prayer**	**Evening Prayer**
Monday	**10 November** *Rw/Gw* Leo the Great, bishop, teacher of the faith, 461 (see p.80) DEL week 32	Wisdom 1.1–7 *or* Titus 1.1–9 Psalm 139.1–9 *or* 24.1–6 Luke 17.1–6	Psalms 19, **20** *or* **1**, 2, 3 Isaiah 5.8–24 Matthew 4.23—5.12	Psalm **34** *or* **4**, 7 Daniel 4.19–end Revelation 5
Tuesday	**11 November** *Rw/Gw* Martin, bishop, c.397 (see p.81)	Wisdom 2.23—3.9 *or* Titus 2.1–8, 11–14 Psalm 34.1–6 *or* 37.3–5, 30–32 Luke 17.7–10	Psalms **21**, 24 *or* **5**, 6 (8) Isaiah 5.25–end Matthew 5.13–20	Psalms 36, **40** *or* **9**, 10* Daniel 5.1–12 Revelation 6
Wednesday	**12 November** *R/G*	Wisdom 6.1–11 *or* Titus 3.1–7 Psalm 82 *or* 23 Luke 17.11–19	Psalms **23**, 25 *or* **119.1–32** Isaiah 6 Matthew 5.21–37	Psalm **37** *or* **11**, 12, 13 Daniel 5.13–end Revelation 7.1–4, 9–end
Thursday	**13 November** *Rw/Gw* Charles Simeon, priest, evangelical divine, 1836 (see p.81)	Wisdom 7.22—8.1 *or* Philemon 7–20 Psalm 119.89–96 *or* 146.4–end Luke 17.20–25	Psalms **26**, 27 *or* 14, **15**, 16 Isaiah 7.1–17 Matthew 5.38–end	Psalms 42, **43** *or* **18*** Daniel 6 Revelation 8
Friday	**14 November** *R/G* *Samuel Seabury, bishop, 1796*	Wisdom 13.1–9 *or* 2 John 4–9 Psalm 19.1–4 *or* 119.1–8 Luke 17.26–end	Psalms 28, **32** *or* 17, **19** Isaiah 8.1–15 Matthew 6.1–18	Psalm **31** *or* **22** Daniel 7.1–14 Revelation 9.1–12
Saturday	**15 November** *R/G*	Wisdom 18.14–16, 19.6–9 *or* 3 John 5–8 Psalm 105.1–5, 35–42 *or* 112 Luke 18.1–8	Psalm **33** *or* 20, 21, **23** Isaiah 8.16—9.7 Matthew 6.19–end	Psalms 84, **86** *or* **24**, 25 Daniel 7.15–end Revelation 9.13–end

2 before Advent

		Principal Service	3rd Service	2nd Service
Sunday	**16 November** *R/G* **2nd Sunday before Advent**	Malachi 4.1–2*a* Psalm 98 2 Thessalonians 3.6–13 Luke 21.5–19	Psalm 132 1 Samuel 16.1–13 Matthew 13.44–52	Psalms [93] 97 Daniel 6 Matthew 13.1–9, 18–23
		Holy Communion	**Morning Prayer**	**Evening Prayer**
Monday	**17 November** *Rw/Gw* Hugh, bishop, 1200 (see p.81) DEL week 33	1 Maccabees 1.10–15, 41–43, 54–57, 62–64 *or* Revelation 1.1–4, 2.1–5 Psalm 79.1–5 *or* 1 Luke 18.35–end	Psalms 46, **47** *or* 27, **30** Isaiah 9.8—10.4 Matthew 7.1–12	Psalms 70, **71** *or* 26, **28**, 29 Daniel 8.1–14 Revelation 10
Tuesday	**18 November** *Rw/Gw* Elizabeth, princess, philanthropist, 1231 (see p.83)	2 Maccabees 6.18–end *or* Revelation 3.1–6, 14–31 Psalm 11 *or* 15 Luke 19.1–10	Psalms 48, **52** *or* 32, **36** Isaiah 10.5–19 Matthew 7.13–end	Psalms **67**, 72 *or* **33** Daniel 8.15–end Revelation 11.1–14
Wednesday	**19 November** *Rw/Gw* Hilda, abbess, 680 (see p.82) *Mechtild, béguine, mystic, 1280*	2 Maccabees 7.1, 20–31 *or* Revelation 4 Psalm 116.10–end *or* 150 Luke 19.11–28	Psalms **56**, 57 *or* **34** Isaiah 10.20–32 Matthew 8.1–13	Psalm **73** *or* **119.33–56** Daniel 9.1–19 Revelation 11.15–end
Thursday	**20 November** *R/Gr* Edmund, king, martyr, 870 (see p.79) *Priscilla Lydia Sellon, a restorer of the religious life in the Church of England, 1876*	1 Maccabees 2.15–29 *or* Revelation 5.1–10 Psalm 129 *or* 149.1–5 Luke 19.41–44	Psalms 61, **62** *or* **37*** Isaiah 10.33—11.9 Matthew 8.14–22	Psalms 74, **76** *or* 39, **40** Daniel 9.20–end Revelation 12
Friday	**21 November** *R/G*	1 Maccabees 4.36–37, 52–59 *or* Revelation 10.8–11 Psalm 122 *or* 119.65–72 Luke 19.45–48	Psalms **63**, 65 *or* **31** Isaiah 11.10—end of 12 Matthew 8.23–end	Psalm **77** *or* **35** Daniel 10.1–11.1 Revelation 13.1–10
Saturday	**22 November** *R/G* *Cecilia, martyr, c.230*	1 Maccabees 6.1–13 *or* Revelation 11.4–12 Psalm 124 *or* 144.1–9 Luke 20.27–40	Psalm **78.1–39** *or* 41, **42**, 43 Isaiah 13.1–13 Matthew 9.1–17	Psalm **78.40–end** *or* 45, **46** Daniel 12 Revelation 13.11–end *or:* 1st EP of Christ the King: Psalms 99, 100; Isaiah 10.33—11.9; 1 Timothy 6.11–16

Christ the King / Sunday next before Advent

			Principal Service	3rd Service	2nd Service
Sunday	**23 November** **Christ the King** *Sunday next before Advent*	*R/W*	Jeremiah 23.1–6 Psalm 46 Colossians 1.11–20 Luke 23.33–43	*MP* Psalms 29, 110 Zechariah 6.9–end Revelation 11.15–18	*EP* Psalm 72 [*or* 72.1–7] 1 Samuel 8.4–20 John 18.33–37
			Holy Communion	**Morning Prayer**	**Evening Prayer**
Monday	**24 November** DEL week 34	*R/G*	Daniel 1.1–6, 8–20 *Canticle:* Bless the Lord Luke 21.1–4	Psalms 92, **96** *or* **44** Isaiah 14.3–20 Matthew 9.18–34	Psalms **80**, 81 *or* **47**, 49 Isaiah 40.1–11 Revelation 14.1–13
Tuesday	**25 November** *Catherine, martyr, 4th cent.* *Isaac Watts, hymn writer, 1748*	*R/G*	Daniel 2.31–45 *Canticle:* Benedicite 1–3 Luke 21.5–11	Psalms **97**, 98, 100 *or* **48**, 52 Isaiah 17 Matthew 9.35—10.15	Psalms 99, **101** *or* **50** Isaiah 40.12–26 Revelation 14.14—end of 15
Wednesday	**26 November**	*R/G*	Daniel 5.1–6, 13–14, 16–17, 23–28 *Canticle:* Benedicite 4–5 Luke 21.12–19	Psalms 110, 111, **112** *or* **119.57–80** Isaiah 19 Matthew 10.16–33	Psalms 121, **122**, 123, 124 *or* **59**, 60 (67) Isaiah 40.27—41.7 Revelation 16.1–11
Thursday	**27 November**	*R/G*	Daniel 6.12–end *Canticle:* Benedicite 6–8*a* Luke 21.20–28	Psalms **125**, 126, 127, 128 *or* 56, **57** (63*) Isaiah 21.1–12 Matthew 10.34—11.1	Psalms 131, 132, **133** *or* 61, **62**, 64 Isaiah 41.8–20 Revelation 16.12–end
Friday	**28 November**	*R/G*	Daniel 7.2–14 *Canticle:* Benedicite 8*b*–10*a* Luke 21.29–33	Psalm **139** *or* **51**, 54 Isaiah 22.1–14 Matthew 11.2–19	Psalms **146**, 147 *or* **38** Isaiah 41.21—42.9 Revelation 17
Saturday	**29 November** *Day of Intercession and Thanksgiving for the Missionary Work of the Church*	*R/G*	Daniel 7.15–27 *Canticle:* Benedicite 10*b*–end Luke 21.34–36	Psalm **145** *or* **68** Isaiah 24 Matthew 11.20–end	Psalms 148, 149, **150** *or* 65, **66** Isaiah 42.10–17 Revelation 18

¶ *Additional Weekday Lectionary*

This Additional Weekday Lectionary provides two readings for each day of the year, except for Sundays, Principal Feasts and other Principal Holy Days, Holy Week and Festivals (for which the readings provided in the main body of this lectionary are used). The readings for 'first evensongs' in the main body of the lectionary are used on the eves of Principal Feasts and may be used on the eves of Festivals. This lectionary is intended particularly for use in those places of worship that attract occasional rather than daily worshippers, and can be used either at Morning or Evening Prayer. Psalmody is not provided and should be taken from the daily provision earlier in this volume.

	1 December – Advent 1		
Monday	**2 December**	Malachi 3.1–6	Matthew 3.1–6
Tuesday	**3 December**	Zephaniah 3.14–end	1 Thessalonians 4.13–end
Wednesday	**4 December**	Isaiah 65.17—66.2	Matthew 24.1–14
Thursday	**5 December**	Micah 5.2–5*a*	John 3.16–21
Friday	**6 December**	Isaiah 66.18–end	Luke 13.22–30
Saturday	**7 December**	Micah 7.8–15	Romans 15.30—16.7, 25–end
	8 December – Advent 2		
Monday	**9 December**	Jeremiah 7.1–11	Philippians 4.4–9
Tuesday	**10 December**	Daniel 7.9–14	Matthew 24.15–28
Wednesday	**11 December**	Amos 9.11–end	Romans 13.8–14
Thursday	**12 December**	Jeremiah 23.5–8	Mark 11.1–11
Friday	**13 December**	Jeremiah 33.14–22	Luke 21.25–36
Saturday	**14 December**	Zechariah 14.4–11	Revelation 22.1–7
	15 December – Advent 3		
Monday	**16 December**	Isaiah 40.1–11	Matthew 3.1–12
Tuesday	**17 December**	Ecclesiasticus 24.1–9 *or* Proverbs 8.22–31	1 Corinthians 2.1–13
Wednesday	**18 December**	Exodus 3.1–6	Acts 7.20–36
Thursday	**19 December**	Isaiah 11.1–9	Romans 15.7–13
Friday	**20 December**	Isaiah 22.21–23	Revelation 3.7–13
Saturday	**21 December**	Numbers 24.15*b*–19	Revelation 22.10–21
	22 December – Advent 4		
Monday	**23 December**	Isaiah 7.10–15	Matthew 1.18–23
Tuesday	**24 December**	*At Evening Prayer the readings for* **Christmas Eve** *are used.* *At other services, the following readings are used:* Isaiah 29.13–18	 1 John 4.7–16
Wednesday	**25 December**	**Christmas Day** – see p.13	
Thursday	**26 December**	Stephen, deacon, martyr – see p.13	
Friday	**27 December**	John, Apostle and Evangelist – see p.13	
Saturday	**28 December**	The Holy Innocents – see p.13	
	29 December – Christmas 1		
Monday	**30 December**	Isaiah 9.2–7	John 8.12–20
Tuesday	**31 December**	Ecclesiastes 3.1–13 *or* 1st EP of Naming and Circumcision of Jesus	Revelation 21.1–8
Wednesday	**1 January**	Naming and Circumcision of Jesus – see p.14	
Thursday	**2 January**	Isaiah 66.6–14	Matthew 12.46–50
Friday	**3 January**	Deuteronomy 6.4–15	John 10.31–end
Saturday	**4 January**	Isaiah 63.7–16 *If, for pastoral reasons,* **The Epiphany** *is celebrated on Sunday 5 January the readings for the Eve of Epiphany are used at Evening Prayer*	Galatians 3.23—4.7

	5 January – Christmas 2 / Epiphany		
Monday	**6 January**	**The Epiphany** – see p.15 *or, if, for pastoral reasons,* **The Epiphany** *is celebrated on Sunday 5 January:* Isaiah 12	 2 Corinthians 2.12–end
Tuesday	**7 January**	Genesis 25.19–end	Ephesians 1.1–6
Wednesday	**8 January**	Joel 2.28–end	Ephesians 1.7–14
Thursday	**9 January**	Proverbs 8.12–21	Ephesians 1.15–end
Friday	**10 January**	Genesis 19.15–29	Ephesians 2.1–10
Saturday	**11 January**	Genesis 17.1–14	Ephesians 2.11–end
	12 January – Baptism of Christ (Epiphany 1)		
Monday	**13 January**	Isaiah 41.14–20	John 1.29–34
Tuesday	**14 January**	Exodus 17.1–7	Acts 8.26–end
Wednesday	**15 January**	Exodus 15.1–19	Colossians 2.8–15
Thursday	**16 January**	Zechariah 6.9–15	1 Peter 2.4–10
Friday	**17 January**	Isaiah 51.7–16	Galatians 6.14–18
Saturday	**18 January**	Leviticus 16.11–22	Hebrews 10.19–25
	19 January – Epiphany 2		
Monday	**20 January**	1 Kings 17.8–16	Mark 8.1–10
Tuesday	**21 January**	1 Kings 19.1–9*a*	Mark 1.9–15
Wednesday	**22 January**	1 Kings 19.9*b*–18	Mark 9.2–13
Thursday	**23 January**	Leviticus 11.1–8, 13–19, 41–45	Acts 10.9–16
Friday	**24 January**	Isaiah 49.8–13 *or* 1st EP of Conversion of Paul	Acts 10.34–43
Saturday	**25 January**	Conversion of Paul – see p.18	
	26 January – Epiphany 3		
Monday	**27 January**	Ezekiel 37.15–end	John 17.1–19
Tuesday	**28 January**	Ezekiel 20.39–44	John 17.20–end
Wednesday	**29 January**	Nehemiah 2.1–10	Romans 12.1–8
Thursday	**30 January**	Deuteronomy 26.16–end	Romans 14.1–9
Friday	**31 January**	Leviticus 19.9–28	Romans 15.1–7
Saturday	**1 February**	Jeremiah 33.1–11 *or* 1st EP of **Presentation of Christ**	1 Peter 5.5*b*–end
	2 February – Presentation		
Monday	**3 February**	Isaiah 42.10–21	Luke 1.5–25
Tuesday	**4 February**	1 Samuel 4.12–end	Luke 1.57–80
Wednesday	**5 February**	Baruch 5 *or* Haggai 1.1–11	Mark 1.1–11
Thursday	**6 February**	Isaiah 35	Matthew 11.2–19
Friday	**7 February**	2 Samuel 11.1–17	Matthew 14.1–12
Saturday	**8 February**	Isaiah 43.15–21	Acts 19.1–10
	9 February – 4 before Lent		
Monday	**10 February**	Genesis 1.26–end	Mark 10.1–16
Tuesday	**11 February**	Ruth 1.1–18	1 John 3.14–end
Wednesday	**12 February**	1 Samuel 1.19*b*–end	Luke 2.41–end
Thursday	**13 February**	Genesis 47.1–12	Ephesians 3.14–end
Friday	**14 February**	2 Samuel 1.17–end	Romans 8.28–end
Saturday	**15 February**	Song of Solomon 2.8–end	1 Corinthians 13
	16 February – 3 before Lent		
Monday	**17 February**	Exodus 23.1–13	James 2.1–13
Tuesday	**18 February**	Deuteronomy 10.12–end	Hebrews 13.1–16
Wednesday	**19 February**	Isaiah 58.6–end	Matthew 25.31–end
Thursday	**20 February**	Isaiah 42.1–9	Luke 4.14–21
Friday	**21 February**	Amos 5.6–15	Ephesians 4.25–end
Saturday	**22 February**	Amos 5.18–24	John 2.13–22

	23 February – 2 before Lent		
Monday	**24 February**	Isaiah 61.1–9	Mark 6.1–13
Tuesday	**25 February**	Isaiah 52.1–10	Romans 10.5–21
Wednesday	**26 February**	Isaiah 52.13—53.6	Romans 15.14–21
Thursday	**27 February**	Isaiah 53.4–12	2 Corinthians 4.1–10
Friday	**28 February**	Zechariah 8.16–end	Matthew 10.1–15
Saturday	**1 March**	Jeremiah 1.4–10	Matthew 10.16–22
	2 March – Sunday next before Lent		
Monday	**3 March**	2 Kings 2.13–22	3 John
Tuesday	**4 March**	Judges 14.5–17	Revelation 10.4–11
Wednesday	**5 March**	**Ash Wednesday** – see p.24	
Thursday	**6 March**	Genesis 2.7–end	Hebrews 2.5–end
Friday	**7 March**	Genesis 4.1–12	Hebrews 4.12–end
Saturday	**8 March**	2 Kings 22.11–end	Hebrews 5.1–10
	9 March – Lent 1		
Monday	**10 March**	Genesis 6.11–end, 7.11–16	Luke 4.14–21
Tuesday	**11 March**	Deuteronomy 31.7–13	1 John 3.1–10
Wednesday	**12 March**	Genesis 11.1–9	Matthew 24.15–28
Thursday	**13 March**	Genesis 13.1–13	1 Peter 2.13–end
Friday	**14 March**	Genesis 21.1–8	Luke 9.18–27
Saturday	**15 March**	Genesis 32.22–32	2 Peter 1.10–end
	16 March – Lent 2		
Monday	**17 March**	1 Chronicles 21.1–17	1 John 2.1–8
Tuesday	**18 March**	Zechariah 3 *or* 1st EP of Joseph of Nazareth	2 Peter 2.1–10*a*
Wednesday	**19 March**	Joseph of Nazareth – see p.26	
Thursday	**20 March**	2 Chronicles 29.1–11	Mark 11.15–19
Friday	**21 March**	Exodus 19.1–9*a*	1 Peter 1.1–9
Saturday	**22 March**	Exodus 19.9*b*–19	Acts 7.44–50
	23 March – Lent 3		
Monday	**24 March**	Joshua 4.1–13 *or* 1st EP of The Annunciation	Luke 9.1–11
Tuesday	**25 March**	**Annunciation of Our Lord to The Blessed Virgin Mary** – see p.27	
Wednesday	**26 March**	Genesis 9.8–17	1 Peter 3.18–end
Thursday	**27 March**	Daniel 12.5–end	Mark 13.21–end
Friday	**28 March**	Numbers 20.1–13	1 Corinthians 10.23–end
Saturday	**29 March**	Isaiah 43.14–end	Hebrews 3.1–15
	30 March – Lent 4		
Monday	**31 March**	2 Kings 24.18—25.7	1 Corinthians 15.20–34
Tuesday	**1 April**	Jeremiah 13.12–19	Acts 13.26–35
Wednesday	**2 April**	Jeremiah 13.20–27	1 Peter 1.17—2.3
Thursday	**3 April**	Jeremiah 22.11–19	Luke 11.37–52
Friday	**4 April**	Jeremiah 17.1–14	Luke 6.17–26
Saturday	**5 April**	Ezra 1	2 Corinthians 1.12–19
	6 April – Lent 5		
Monday	**7 April**	Joel 2.12–17	2 John
Tuesday	**8 April**	Isaiah 58.1–14	Mark 10.32–45
Wednesday	**9 April**	Job 36.1–12	John 14.1–14
Thursday	**10 April**	Jeremiah 9.17–22	Luke 13.31–35
Friday	**11 April**	Lamentations 5.1–3,19–22	John 12.20–26
Saturday	**12 April**	Job 17.6–end	John 12.27–36

From the Monday of Holy Week until Easter Eve the Seasonal Lectionary Is used: see pp.30–31

	20 April – Easter		
Monday	**21 April**	Isaiah 54.1–14	Romans 1.1–7
Tuesday	**22 April**	Isaiah 51.1–11	John 5.19–29
Wednesday	**23 April**	Isaiah 26.1–19	John 20.1–10
Thursday	**24 April**	Isaiah 43.14–21	Revelation 1.4–end
Friday	**25 April**	Isaiah 42.10–17	1 Thessalonians 5.1–11
Saturday	**26 April**	Job 14.1–14	John 21.1–14
	27 April – Easter 2		
Monday	**28 April**	George, martyr, patron of England – see p.33	
Tuesday	**29 April**	Mark the Evangelist – see p.33	
Wednesday	**30 April**	Hosea 5.15—6.6 *or* 1st EP of Philip and James, Apostles	1 Corinthians 15.1–11
Thursday	**1 May**	Philip and James, Apostles – see p.33	
Friday	**2 May**	Genesis 6.9–end	1 Peter 3.8–end
Saturday	**3 May**	1 Samuel 2.1–8	Matthew 28.8–15
	4 May – Easter 3		
Monday	**5 May**	Exodus 24.1–11	Revelation 5
Tuesday	**6 May**	Leviticus 19.9–18, 32–end	Matthew 5.38–end
Wednesday	**7 May**	Genesis 3.8–21	1 Corinthians 15.12–28
Thursday	**8 May**	Isaiah 33.13–22	Mark 6.47–end
Friday	**9 May**	Nehemiah 9.6–17	Romans 5.12–end
Saturday	**10 May**	Isaiah 61.10—62.5	Luke 24.1–12
	11 May – Easter 4		
Monday	**12 May**	Jeremiah 31.10–17	Revelation 7.9–end
Tuesday	**13 May**	Job 31.13–23 *or* 1st EP of Matthias the Apostle	Matthew 7.1–12
Wednesday	**14 May**	Matthias the Apostle – see p.35	
Thursday	**15 May**	Proverbs 28.3–end	Mark 10.17–31
Friday	**16 May**	Ecclesiastes 12.1–8	Romans 6.1–11
Saturday	**17 May**	1 Chronicles 29.10–13	Luke 24.13–35
	18 May – Easter 5		
Monday	**19 May**	Genesis 15.1–18	Romans 4.13–end
Tuesday	**20 May**	Deuteronomy 8.1–10	Matthew 6.19–end
Wednesday	**21 May**	Hosea 13.4–14	1 Corinthians 15.50–end
Thursday	**22 May**	Exodus 3.1–15	Mark 12.18–27
Friday	**23 May**	Ezekiel 36.33–end	Romans 8.1–11
Saturday	**24 May**	Isaiah 38.9–20	Luke 24.33–end
	25 May – Easter 6		
Monday	**26 May**	Proverbs 4.1–13	Philippians 2.1–11
Tuesday	**27 May**	Isaiah 32.12–end	Romans 5.1–11
Wednesday	**28 May**	*At Evening Prayer the readings for the Eve of Ascension Day are used. At other services, the following readings are used:* Isaiah 43.1–13	Titus 2.11—3.8
Thursday	**29 May**	**Ascension Day** – see p.38	
Friday	**30 May**	Exodus 35.30—36.1 *or* 1st EP of Visit of the Blessed Virgin Mary to Elizabeth	Galatians 5.13–end
Saturday	**31 May**	Visit of the Blessed Virgin Mary to Elizabeth – see p.38	
	1 June – Easter 7		
Monday	**2 June**	Numbers 27.15–end	1 Corinthians 3
Tuesday	**3 June**	1 Samuel 10.1–10	1 Corinthians 12.1–13
Wednesday	**4 June**	1 Kings 19.1–18	Matthew 3.13–end
Thursday	**5 June**	Ezekiel 11.14–20	Matthew 9.35—10.20
Friday	**6 June**	Ezekiel 36.22–28	Matthew 12.22–32
Saturday	**7 June**	*At Evening Prayer the readings for the Eve of Pentecost are used. At other services, the following readings are used:* Micah 3.1–8	Ephesians 6.10–20

	8 June – Pentecost		
Monday	**9 June**	Genesis 12.1–9	Romans 4.13–end
Tuesday	**10 June**	Genesis 13.1–12	Romans 12.9–end
		or 1st EP of Barnabas the Apostle	
Wednesday	**11 June**	Barnabas the Apostle – see p.40	
Thursday	**12 June**	Genesis 22.1–18	Hebrews 11.8–19
Friday	**13 June**	Isaiah 51.1–8	John 8.48–end
Saturday	**14 June**	*At Evening Prayer the readings for the Eve of Trinity Sunday are used. At other services, the following readings are used:*	
		Ecclesiasticus 44.19–23	James 2.14–26
		or Joshua 2.1–15	
	15 June – Trinity Sunday		
Monday	**16 June**	Exodus 2.1–10	Hebrews 11.23–31
Tuesday	**17 June**	Exodus 2.11–end	Acts 7.17–29
Wednesday	**18 June**	Exodus 3.1–12	Acts 7.30–38
		or 1st EP of Corpus Christi	
Thursday	**19 June**	Day of Thanksgiving for the Institution of the Holy Communion (Corpus Christi) – see p.41	
		Or, where Corpus Christi *is celebrated as a Lesser Festival:*	
		Exodus 6.1–13	John 9.24–38
Friday	**20 June**	Exodus 34.1–10	Mark 7.1–13
Saturday	**21 June**	Exodus 34.27–end	2 Corinthians 3.7–end
	22 June – Trinity 1		
Monday	**23 June**	Genesis 37.1–11	Romans 11.9–21
		or 1st EP of Birth of John the Baptist	
Tuesday	**24 June**	Birth of John the Baptist – see p.42	
Wednesday	**25 June**	Genesis 42.17–end	Matthew 18.1–14
Thursday	**26 June**	Genesis 45.1–15	Acts 7.9–16
Friday	**27 June**	Genesis 47.1–12	1 Thessalonians 5.12–end
Saturday	**28 June**	Genesis 50.4–21	Luke 15.11–end
		or 1st EP of Peter and Paul	
	29 June – Trinity 2		
Monday	**30 June**	Isaiah 32	James 3.13–end
Tuesday	**1 July**	Proverbs 3.1–18	Matthew 5.1–12
Wednesday	**2 July**	Judges 6.1–16	Matthew 5.13–24
		or 1st EP of Thomas the Apostle	
Thursday	**3 July**	Thomas the Apostle – see p.44	
		If Thomas the Apostle *is celebrated on 21 December, the following readings are used:*	
		Jeremiah 6.9–15	1 Timothy 2.1–6
Friday	**4 July**	1 Samuel 16.14–end	John 14.15–end
Saturday	**5 July**	Isaiah 6.1–9	Revelation 19.9–end
	6 July – Trinity 3		
Monday	**7 July**	Exodus 13.13*b*–end	Luke 15.1–10
Tuesday	**8 July**	Proverbs 1.20–end	James 5.13–end
Wednesday	**9 July**	Isaiah 5.8–24	James 1.17–25
Thursday	**10 July**	Isaiah 57.14–end	John 13.1–17
Friday	**11 July**	Jeremiah 15.15–end	Luke 16.19–31
Saturday	**12 July**	Isaiah 25.1–9	Acts 2.22–33
	13 July – Trinity 4		
Monday	**14 July**	Exodus 20.1–17	Matthew 6.1–15
Tuesday	**15 July**	Proverbs 6.6–19	Luke 4.1–14
Wednesday	**16 July**	Isaiah 24.1–15	1 Corinthians 6.1–11
Thursday	**17 July**	Job 7	Matthew 7.21–29
Friday	**18 July**	Jeremiah 20.7–end	Matthew 27.27–44
Saturday	**19 July**	Job 28	Hebrews 11.32—12.2

	20 July – Trinity 5		
Monday	**21 July**	Exodus 32.1–14 *or* 1st EP of Mary Magdalene	Colossians 3.1–11
Tuesday	**22 July**	Mary Magdalene – see p.47	
Wednesday	**23 July**	Isaiah 26.1–9	Romans 8.12–27
Thursday	**24 July**	Jeremiah 8.18—9.6 *or* 1st EP of James the Apostle	John 13.21–35
Friday	**25 July**	James the Apostle – see p.47	
Saturday	**26 July**	Hosea 11.1–11	Matthew 28.1–7
	27 July – Trinity 6		
Monday	**28 July**	Exodus 40.1–16	Luke 14.15–24
Tuesday	**29 July**	Proverbs 11.1–12	Mark 12.38–44
Wednesday	**30 July**	Isaiah 33.2–10	Philippians 1.1–11
Thursday	**31 July**	Job 38	Luke 18.1–14
Friday	**1 August**	Job 42.1–6	John 3.1–15
Saturday	**2 August**	Ecclesiastes 9.1–11	Hebrews 1.1–9
	3 August – Trinity 7		
Monday	**4 August**	Numbers 23.1–12	1 Corinthians 1.10–17
Tuesday	**5 August**	Proverbs 12.1–12 *or* 1st EP of Transfiguration of Our Lord	Galatians 3.1–14
Wednesday	**6 August**	Transfiguration of Our Lord – see p.49	
Thursday	**7 August**	Hosea 14	John 15.1–17
Friday	**8 August**	2 Samuel 18.18–end	Matthew 27.57–66
Saturday	**9 August**	Isaiah 55.1–7	Mark 16.1–8
	10 August – Trinity 8		
Monday	**11 August**	Joel 3.16–21	Mark 4.21–34
Tuesday	**12 August**	Proverbs 12.13–end	John 1.43–51
Wednesday	**13 August**	Isaiah 55.8–end	2 Timothy 2.8–19
Thursday	**14 August**	Isaiah 38.1–8 *or* 1st EP of The Blessed Virgin Mary	Mark 5.21–43
Friday	**15 August**	The Blessed Virgin Mary – see p.50 *If* The Blessed Virgin Mary *is celebrated on 8 September, the following readings are used:* Jeremiah 14.1–9	 Luke 8.4–15
Saturday	**16 August**	Ecclesiastes 5.10–19	1 Timothy 6.6–16
	17 August – Trinity 9		
Monday	**18 August**	Joshua 1.1–9	1 Corinthians 9.19–end
Tuesday	**19 August**	Proverbs 15.1–11	Galatians 2.15–end
Wednesday	**20 August**	Isaiah 49.1–7	1 John 1
Thursday	**21 August**	Proverbs 27.1–12	John 15.12–27
Friday	**22 August**	Isaiah 59.8–end	Mark 15.6–20
Saturday	**23 August**	Zechariah 7.8—8.8 *or* 1st EP of Bartholomew the Apostle	Luke 20.27–40
	24 August – Bartholomew the Apostle / Trinity 10		
Monday	**25 August**	Judges 13.1–23 *or* Bartholomew the Apostle transferred – see p.52	Luke 10.38–42
Tuesday	**26 August**	Proverbs 15.15–end	Matthew 15.21–28
Wednesday	**27 August**	Isaiah 45.1–7	Ephesians 4.1–16
Thursday	**28 August**	Jeremiah 16.1–15	Luke 12.35–48
Friday	**29 August**	Jeremiah 18.1–11	Hebrews 1.1–9
Saturday	**30 August**	Jeremiah 26.1–19	Ephesians 3.1–13
	31 August – Trinity 11		
Monday	**1 September**	Ruth 2.1–13	Luke 10.25–37
Tuesday	**2 September**	Proverbs 16.1–11	Philippians 3.4*b*–end
Wednesday	**3 September**	Deuteronomy 11.1–21	2 Corinthians 9.6–end
Thursday	**4 September**	Ecclesiasticus 2 *or* Ecclesiastes 2.12–25	John 16.1–15
Friday	**5 September**	Obadiah 1–10	John 19.1–16
Saturday	**6 September**	2 Kings 2.11–14	Luke 24.36–end

	7 September – Trinity 12		
Monday	**8 September**	1 Samuel 17.32–50	Matthew 8.14–22
Tuesday	**9 September**	Proverbs 17.1–15	Luke 7.1–17
Wednesday	**10 September**	Jeremiah 5.20–end	2 Peter 3.8–end
Thursday	**11 September**	Daniel 2.1–23	Luke 10.1–20
Friday	**12 September**	Daniel 3.1–28	Revelation 15
Saturday	**13 September**	Daniel 6 *or* 1st EP of Holy Cross Day	Philippians 2.14–24
	14 September – Holy Cross Day / Trinity 13		
Monday	**15 September**	2 Samuel 7.4–17 *or* Holy Cross Day transferred – see p.56	2 Corinthians 5.1–10
Tuesday	**16 September**	Proverbs 18.10–21	Romans 14.10–end
Wednesday	**17 September**	Judges 4.1–10	Romans 1.8–17
Thursday	**18 September**	Isaiah 49.14–end	John 16.16–24
Friday	**19 September**	Job 9.1–24	Mark 15.21–32
Saturday	**20 September**	Exodus 19.1–9 *or* 1st EP of Matthew, Apostle and Evangelist	John 20.11–18
	21 September – Matthew, Apostle and Evangelist / Trinity 14		
Monday	**22 September**	Haggai 1 *or* Matthew, Apostle and Evangelist transferred – see p.58	Mark 7.9–23
Tuesday	**23 September**	Proverbs 21.1–18	Mark 6.30–44
Wednesday	**24 September**	Hosea 11.1–11	1 John 4.9–end
Thursday	**25 September**	Lamentations 3.34–48	Romans 7.14–end
Friday	**26 September**	2 Kings 19.4–18	1 Thessalonians 3
Saturday	**27 September**	Ecclesiasticus 4.11–28 *or* Deuteronomy 29.2–15	2 Timothy 3.10–end
	28 September – Trinity 15		
Monday	**29 September**	Michael and All Angels – see p.60	
Tuesday	**30 September**	Proverbs 8.1–11	Luke 6.39–end
Wednesday	**1 October**	Proverbs 2.1–15	Colossians 1.9–20
Thursday	**2 October**	Baruch 3.14–end *or* Genesis 1.1–13	John 1.1–18
Friday	**3 October**	Ecclesiasticus 1.1–20 *or* Deuteronomy 7.7–16	1 Corinthians 1.18–end
Saturday	**4 October**	Wisdom 9.1–12 *or* Jeremiah 1.4–10	Luke 2.41–end
	5 October – Trinity 16		
Monday	**6 October**	Genesis 21.1–13	Luke 1.26–38
Tuesday	**7 October**	Ruth 4.7–17	Luke 2.25–38
Wednesday	**8 October**	2 Kings 4.1–7	John 2.1–11
Thursday	**9 October**	2 Kings 4.25*b*–37	Mark 3.19*b*–35
Friday	**10 October**	Judith 8.9–17, 28–36 *or* Ruth 1.1–18	John 19.25*b*–30
Saturday	**11 October**	Exodus 15.19–27	Acts 1.6–14
	12 October – Trinity 17		
Monday	**13 October**	Exodus 19.16–end	Hebrews 12.18–end
Tuesday	**14 October**	1 Chronicles 16.1–13	Revelation 11.15–end
Wednesday	**15 October**	1 Chronicles 29.10–19	Colossians 3.12–17
Thursday	**16 October**	Nehemiah 8.1–12	1 Corinthians 14.1–12
Friday	**17 October**	Isaiah 1.10–17 *or* 1st EP of Luke the Evangelist	Mark 12.28–34
Saturday	**18 October**	Luke the Evangelist – see p.62	

	19 October – Trinity 18		
Monday	**20 October**	2 Samuel 22.4–7, 17–20	Hebrews 7.26—8.6
Tuesday	**21 October**	Proverbs 22.17–end	2 Corinthians 12.1–10
Wednesday	**22 October**	Hosea 14	James 2.14–26
Thursday	**23 October**	Isaiah 24.1–15	John 16.25–33
Friday	**24 October**	Jeremiah 14.1–9	Luke 23.44–56
Saturday	**25 October**	Zechariah 8.14–end	John 20.19–end
	26 October – Last after Trinity		
Monday	**27 October**	Isaiah 42.14–21 *or* 1st EP of Simon and Jude, Apostles	Luke 1.5–25
Tuesday	**28 October**	Simon and Jude, Apostles – see p.64	
Wednesday	**29 October**	Baruch 5 *or* Haggai 1.1–11	Mark 1.1–11
Thursday	**30 October**	Isaiah 35	Matthew 11.2–19
Friday	**31 October**	2 Samuel 11.1–17 *or* 1st EP of **All Saints' Day**	Matthew 14.1–12
Saturday	**1 November**	**All Saints' Day** – see p.65 *or, if* **All Saints' Day** *is celebrated on Sunday 2 November only, at Evening Prayer the readings for the Eve of All Saints' Day are used. At other services, the following readings are used:* Isaiah 43.15–21	Acts 19.1–10
	2 November – 4 before Advent / All Saints' Day		
Monday	**3 November**	Esther 3.1–11, 4.7–17	Matthew 18.1–10
Tuesday	**4 November**	Ezekiel 18.21–end	Matthew 18.12–20
Wednesday	**5 November**	Proverbs 3.27–end	Matthew 18.21–end
Thursday	**6 November**	Exodus 23.1–9	Matthew 19.1–15
Friday	**7 November**	Proverbs 3.13–18	Matthew 19.16–end
Saturday	**8 November**	Deuteronomy 28.1–6	Matthew 20.1–16
	9 November – 3 before Advent (Remembrance Sunday)		
Monday	**10 November**	Isaiah 40.21–end	Romans 11.25–end
Tuesday	**11 November**	Ezekiel 34.20–end	John 10.1–18
Wednesday	**12 November**	Leviticus 26.3–13	Titus 2.1–10
Thursday	**13 November**	Hosea 6.1–6	Matthew 9.9–13
Friday	**14 November**	Malachi 4	John 4.5–26
Saturday	**15 November**	Micah 6.6–8	Colossians 3.12–17
	16 November – 2 before Advent		
Monday	**17 November**	Micah 7.1–7	Matthew 10.24–39
Tuesday	**18 November**	Habakkuk 3.1–19*a*	1 Corinthians 4.9–16
Wednesday	**19 November**	Zechariah 8.1–13	Mark 13.3–8
Thursday	**20 November**	Zechariah 10.6–end	1 Peter 5.1–11
Friday	**21 November**	Micah 4.1–5	Luke 9.28–36
Saturday	**22 November**	*At Evening Prayer the readings for the Eve of Christ the King are used. At other services, the following readings are used:* Exodus 16.1–21	John 6.3–15
	23 November – Christ the King (Sunday next before Advent)		
Monday	**24 November**	Jeremiah 30.1–3, 10–17	Romans 12.9–21
Tuesday	**25 November**	Jeremiah 30.18–24	John 10.22–30
Wednesday	**26 November**	Jeremiah 31.1–9	Matthew 15.21–31
Thursday	**27 November**	Jeremiah 31.10–17	Matthew 16.13–end
Friday	**28 November**	Jeremiah 31.31–37	Hebrews 10.11–18
Saturday	**29 November**	Isaiah 51.17—52.2	Ephesians 5.1–20

¶ *Collects and Post Communions*

All the contemporary language Collects and Post Communions, including the Additional Collects, may be found in *Common Worship: Collects and Post Communions* (Church House Publishing: London, 2004). The Additional Collects are also published separately.

The contemporary language Collects and Post Communions all appear in *Times and Seasons: President's Edition for Holy Communion*. Apart from the Additional Collects, they appear in the other Common Worship volumes as follows:

- ¶ President's edition: all Collects and Post Communions;
- ¶ *Daily Prayer*: all Collects;
- ¶ main volume: Collects, Additional Collects and Post Communions for Sundays, Principal Feasts and Holy Days, and Festivals;
- ¶ *Festivals*: Collects and Post Communions for Festivals, Lesser Festivals, Common of the Saints and Special Occasions.

The traditional-language Collects and Post Communions all appear in the president's edition. They appear in other publications as follows:

- ¶ main volume: Collects and Post Communions for Sundays, Principal Feasts and Holy Days, and Festivals;
- ¶ separate booklet: Collects and Post Communions for Lesser Festivals, Common of the Saints and Special Occasions.

¶ *Lectionary for Dedication Festival*

If date not known, observe on the first Sunday in October or Last Sunday after Trinity.

Evening Prayer on the Eve

Psalm 24
2 Chronicles 7.11–16
John 4.19–29

Dedication Festival

Gold or White

	Principal Service	3rd Service	2nd Service	Psalmody
Year A	1 Kings 8.22–30 *or* Revelation 21.9–14 Psalm 122 Hebrews 12.18–24 Matthew 21.12–16	Haggai 2.6–9 Hebrews 10.19–25	Jeremiah 7.1–11 1 Corinthians 3.9–17 *HC* Luke 19.1–10	*MP* 48, 150 *EP* 132
Year B	Genesis 28.11–18 *or* Revelation 21.9–14 Psalm 122 1 Peter 2.1–10 John 10.22–29	Haggai 2.6–9 Hebrews 10.19–25	Jeremiah 7.1–11 Luke 19.1–10	*MP* 48, 150 *EP* 132
Year C	1 Chronicles 29.6–19 Psalm 122 Ephesians 2.19–end John 2.13–22	Haggai 2.6–9 Hebrews 10.19–25	Jeremiah 7.1–11 Luke 19.1–10	*MP* 48, 150 *EP* 132

¶ *Lectionary for Common of the Saints*

The Blessed Virgin Mary

Genesis 3.8–15, 20; Isaiah 7.10–14; Micah 5.1–4
Psalms 45.10–17; 113; 131
Acts 1.12–14; Romans 8.18–30; Galatians 4.4–7
Luke 1.26–38; *or* 1.39–47; John 19.25–27

Martyrs

2 Chronicles 24.17–21; Isaiah 43.1–7; Jeremiah 11.18–20; Wisdom 4.10–15
Psalms 3; 11; 31.1–5; 44.18–24; 126
Romans 8.35–end; 2 Corinthians 4.7–15; 2 Timothy 2.3–7 [8–13]; Hebrews 11.32–end; 1 Peter 4.12–end; Revelation 12.10–12*a*
Matthew 10.16–22; *or* 10.28–39; *or* 16.24–26; John 12.24–26; *or* 15.18–21

Agnes (21 Jan): *also* Revelation 7.13–end
Alban (22 June): *especially* 2 Timothy 2.3–13; John 12.24–26
Alphege (19 Apr): *also* Hebrews 5.1–4
Boniface (5 June): *also* Acts 20.24–28
Charles (30 Jan): *also* Ecclesiasticus 2.12–end; 1 Timothy 6.12–16
Clement (23 Nov): *also* Philippians 3.17—4.3; Matthew 16.13–19
Cyprian (15 Sept): *especially* 1 Peter 4.12–end; *also* Matthew 18.18–22
Edmund (20 Nov): *also* Proverbs 20.28; 21.1–4, 7
Ignatius (17 Oct): *also* Philippians 3.7–12; John 6.52–58
James Hannington (29 Oct): *especially* Matthew 10.28–39
Janani Luwum (17 Feb): *also* Ecclesiasticus 4.20–28; John 12.24–32
John Coleridge Patteson (20 Sept): *especially* 2 Chronicles 24.17–21; *also* Acts 7.55–end
Justin (1 June): *especially* John 15.18–21; *also* 1 Maccabees 2.15–22; 1 Corinthians 1.18–25
Laurence (10 Aug): *also* 2 Corinthians 9.6–10
Lucy (13 Dec): *also* Wisdom 3.1–7; 2 Corinthians 4.6–15
Oswald (5 Aug): *especially* 1 Peter 4.12–end; John 16.29–end
Perpetua, Felicity and comps (7 Mar): *especially* Revelation 12.10–12*a*; *also* Wisdom 3.1–7
Polycarp (23 Feb): *also* Revelation 2.8–11
Thomas Becket (29 Dec *or* 7 Jul): *especially* Matthew 10.28–33; *also* Ecclesiasticus 51.1–8
William Tyndale (6 Oct): *also* Proverbs 8.4–11; 2 Timothy 3.12–end

Teachers of the Faith and Spiritual Writers

1 Kings 3.[6–10] 11–14; Proverbs 4.1–9; Wisdom 7.7–10, 15–16; Ecclesiasticus 39.1–10
Psalms 19.7–10; 34.11–17; 37.31–35; 119.89–96; 119.97–104
1 Corinthians 1.18–25; *or* 2.1–10; *or* 2.9–end; Ephesians 3.8–12; 2 Timothy 4.1–8; Titus 2.1–8
Matthew 5.13–19; *or* 13.52–end; *or* 23.8–12; Mark 4.1–9; John 16.12–15

Ambrose (7 Dec): *also* Isaiah 41.9*b*–13; Luke 22.24–30
Anselm (21 Apr): *also* Wisdom 9.13–end; Romans 5.8–11
Athanasius (2 May): *also* Ecclesiasticus 4.20–28; *also* Matthew 10.24–27
Augustine of Hippo (28 Aug): *especially* Ecclesiasticus 39.1–10; *also* Romans 13.11–13
Basil and Gregory (2 Jan): *especially* 2 Timothy 4.1–8; Matthew 5.13–19
Bernard (20 Aug): *especially* Revelation 19.5–9
Catherine of Siena (29 Apr): *also* Proverbs 8.1, 6–11; John 17.12–end
Francis de Sales (24 Jan): *also* Proverbs 3.13–18; John 3.17–21
Gregory the Great (3 Sept): *also* 1 Thessalonians 2.3–8
Gregory of Nyssa and Macrina (19 July): *especially* 1 Corinthians 2.9–13; *also* Wisdom 9.13–17
Hilary (13 Jan): *also* 1 John 2.18–25; John 8.25–32
Irenaeus (28 June): *also* 2 Peter 1.16–end
Jeremy Taylor (13 Aug); *also* Titus 2.7–8, 11–14
John Bunyan (30 Aug): *also* Hebrews 12.1–2; Luke 21.21, 34–36
John Chrysostom (13 Sept): *especially* Matthew 5.13–19; *also* Jeremiah 1.4–10
John of the Cross (14 Dec): *especially* 1 Corinthians 2.1–10; *also* John 14.18–23
Leo (10 Nov): *also* 1 Peter 5.1–11
Richard Hooker (3 Nov): *especially* John 16.12–15; *also* Ecclesiasticus 44.10–15
Teresa of Avila (15 Oct): *also* Romans 8.22–27
Thomas Aquinas (28 Jan): *especially* Wisdom 7.7–10, 15–16; 1 Corinthians 2.9–end; John 16.12–15
William Law (10 Apr): *especially* 1 Corinthians 2.9–end; *also* Matthew 17.1–9

Bishops and Other Pastors

1 Samuel 16.1, 6–13; Isaiah 6.1–8; Jeremiah 1.4–10; Ezekiel 3.16–21; Malachi 2.5–7
Psalms 1; 15; 16.5–end; 96; 110
Acts 20.28–35; 1 Corinthians 4.1–5; 2 Corinthians 4.1–10 [*or* 1–2, 5–7];
or 5.14–20; 1 Peter 5.1–4
Matthew 11.25–end; *or* 24.42–46; John 10.11–16; *or* 15.9–17; *or* 21.15–17

Augustine of Canterbury (26 May): *also* 1 Thessalonians 2.2*b*–8; Matthew 13.31–33
Charles Simeon (13 Nov): *especially* Malachi 2.5–7; *also* Colossians 1.3–8; Luke 8.4–8
David (1 Mar): *also* 2 Samuel 23.1–4; Psalm 89.19–22, 24
Dunstan (19 May): *especially* Matthew 24.42–46; *also* Exodus 31.1–5
Edward King (8 Mar): *also* Hebrews 13.1–8
George Herbert (27 Feb): *especially* Malachi 2.5–7; Matthew 11.25–end;
also Revelation 19.5–9
Hugh (17 Nov); *also* 1 Timothy 6.11–16
John Keble (14 July): *also* Lamentations 3.19–26; Matthew 5.1–8
John and Charles Wesley (24 May): *also* Ephesians 5.15–20
Lancelot Andrewes (25 Sept): *especially* Isaiah 6.1–8
Martin of Tours (11 Nov): *also* 1 Thessalonians 5.1–11; Matthew 25.34–40
Nicholas (6 Dec): *also* Isaiah 61.1–3; 1 Timothy 6.6–11; Mark 10.13–16
Richard (16 June): *also* John 21.15–19
Swithun (15 July): *also* James 5.7–11, 13–18
Thomas Ken (8 June): *especially* 2 Corinthians 4.1–10 [*or* 1–2, 5–7]; Matthew 24.42–46
Wulfstan (19 Jan): *especially* Matthew 24.42–46

Members of Religious Communities

1 Kings 19.9–18; Proverbs 10.27–end; Song of Solomon 8.6–7; Isaiah 61.10—62.5; Hosea 2.14–15, 19–20

Psalms 34.1–8; 112.1–9; 119.57–64; 123; 131

Acts 4.32–35; 2 Corinthians 10.17—11.2; Philippians 3.7–14; 1 John 2.15–17; Revelation 19.1, 5–9

Matthew 11.25–end; *or* 19.3–12; *or* 19.23–end; Luke 9.57–end; *or* 12.32–37

Aelred (12 Jan): *also* Ecclesiasticus 15.1–6
Alcuin (20 May): *also* Colossians 3.12–16; John 4.19–24
Antony (17 Jan): *especially* Philippians 3.7–14, *also* Matthew 19.16–26
Bede (25 May): *also* Ecclesiasticus 39.1–10
Benedict (11 July): *also* 1 Corinthians 3.10–11; Luke 18.18–22
Clare (11 Aug): *especially* Song of Solomon 8.6–7
Dominic (8 Aug): *also* Ecclesiasticus 39.1–10
Etheldreda (23 June): *also* Matthew 25.1–13
Francis of Assisi (4 Oct): *also* Galatians 6.14–end; Luke 12.22–34
Hilda (19 Nov): *especially* Isaiah 61.10—62.5
Hildegard (17 Sept): *also* 1 Corinthians 2.9–13; Luke 10.21–24
Julian of Norwich (8 May): *also* 1 Corinthians 13.8–end; Matthew 5.13–16
Vincent de Paul (27 Sept): *also* 1 Corinthians 1.25–end; Matthew 25.34–40

Missionaries

Isaiah 52.7–10; *or* 61.1–3*a*; Ezekiel 34.11–16; Jonah 3.1–5

Psalms 67; *or* 87; *or* 97; *or* 100; *or* 117

Acts 2.14, 22–36; *or* 13.46–49; *or* 16.6–10; *or* 26.19–23; Romans 15.17–21; 2 Corinthians 5.11—6.2

Matthew 9.35–end; *or* 28.16–end; Mark 16.15–20; Luke 5.1–11; *or* 10.1–9

Aidan (31 Aug): *also* 1 Corinthians 9.16–19
Anskar (3 Feb): *especially* Isaiah 52.7–10; *also* Romans 10.11–15
Chad (2 Mar *or* 26 Oct): *also* 1 Timothy 6.11*b*–16
Columba (9 June): *also* Titus 2.11–end
Cuthbert (20 Mar *or* 4 Sept): *especially* Ezekiel 34.11–16; *also* Matthew 18.12–14
Cyril and Methodius (14 Feb): *especially* Isaiah 52.7–10; *also* Romans 10.11–15
Henry Martyn (19 Oct): *especially* Mark 16.15–end; *also* Isaiah 55.6–11
Ninian (16 Sept): *especially* Acts 13.46–49; Mark 16.15–end
Patrick (17 Mar): *also* Psalm 91.1–4, 13–end; Luke 10.1–12, 17–20
Paulinus (10 Oct); *especially* Matthew 28.16–end
Wilfrid (12 Oct): *especially* Luke 5.1–11; *also* 1 Corinthians 1.18–25
Willibrord (7 Nov): *especially* Isaiah 52.7–10; Matthew 28.16–end

Any Saint

General

Genesis 12.1–4; Proverbs 8.1–11; Micah 6.6–8; Ecclesiasticus 2.7–13 [14–end]
Psalms 32; 33.1–5; 119.1–8; 139.1–4 [5–12]; 145.8–14
Ephesians 3.14–19; *or* 6.11–18; Hebrews 13.7–8, 15–16; James 2.14–17;
1 John 4.7–16; Revelation 21.[1–4] 5–7
Matthew 19.16–21; *or* 25.1–13; *or* 25.14–30; John 15.1–8; *or* 17.20–end

Christian rulers

1 Samuel 16.1–13*a*; 1 Kings 3.3–14
Psalms 72.1–7; 99
1 Timothy 2.1–6
Mark 10.42–45; Luke 14.27–33

Alfred the Great (26 Oct): *also* 2 Samuel 23.1–5; John 18.33–37
Edward the Confessor (13 Oct): *also* 2 Samuel 23.1–5; 1 John 4.13–16
Margaret of Scotland (16 Nov): *also* Proverbs 31.10–12, 20, 26–end;
1 Corinthians 12.13—13.3; Matthew 25.34–end

Those working for the poor and underprivileged

Isaiah 58.6–11
Psalms 82; 146.5–10
Hebrews 13.1–3; 1 John 3.14–18
Matthew 5.1–12; *or* 25.31–end

Elizabeth of Hungary (18 Nov): *especially* Matthew 25.31–end; *also* Proverbs 31.10–end
Josephine Butler (30 May): *especially* Isaiah 58.6–11; *also* 1 John 3.18–23; Matthew 9.10–13
William Wilberforce, Olaudah Equiano and Thomas Clarkson (30 July): *also* Job 31.16–23;
Galatians 3.26–end, 4.6–7; Luke 4.16–21

Men and women of learning

Proverbs 8.22–31; Ecclesiasticus 44.1–15
Psalms 36.5–10; 49.1–4
Philippians 4.7–8
Matthew 13.44–46, 52; John 7.14–18

Those whose holiness was revealed in marriage and family life

Proverbs 31.10–13, 19–20, 30–end; Tobit 8.4–7
Psalms 127; 128
1 Peter 3.1–9
Mark 3.31–end; Luke 10.38–end

Mary Sumner (9 Aug): *also* Hebrews 13.1–5
Monica (27 Aug): *also* Ecclesiasticus 26.1–3, 13–16

The Guidance of the Holy Spirit

Proverbs 24.3–7; Isaiah 30.15–21; Wisdom 9.13–17
Psalms 25.1–9; 104.26–33; 143.8–10
Acts 15.23–29; Romans 8:22–27; 1 Corinthians 12.4–13
Luke 14.27–33; John 14.23–26; *or* 16.13–15

Rogation Days

(26–28 May in 2025)

Deuteronomy 8.1–10; 1 Kings 8.35–40; Job 28.1–11
Psalms 104.21–30; 107.1–9; 121
Philippians 4.4–7; 2 Thessalonians 3.6–13; 1 John 5.12–15
Matthew 6.1–15; Mark 11.22–24; Luke 11.5–13

Harvest Thanksgiving

Year A
Deuteronomy 8.7–18 *or* 28.1–14
Psalm 65
2 Corinthians 9.6–end
Luke 12.16–30; *or* 17.11–19

Year B
Joel 2.21–27
Psalm 126
1 Timothy 2.1–7; *or* 6.6–10
Matthew 6.25–33

Year C
Deuteronomy 26.1–11
Psalm 100
Philippians 4.4–9
or Revelation 14.14–18
John 6.25–35

Mission and Evangelism

Isaiah 49.1–6; *or* 52.7–10; Micah 4.1–5
Psalms 2; 46; 67
Acts 17.10–end; 2 Corinthians 5.14—6.2; Ephesians 2.13–end
Matthew 5.13–16; *or* 28.16–end; John 17.20–end

The Unity of the Church

Jeremiah 33.6–9*a*; Ezekiel 36.23–28; Zephaniah 3.16–end
Psalms 100; 122; 133
Ephesians 4.1–6; Colossians 3.9–17; 1 John 4.9–15
Matthew 18.19–22; John 11.45–52; *or* 17.11*b*–23

The Peace of the World

Isaiah 9.1–6; *or* 57.15–19; Micah 4.1–5
Psalms 40.14–17; 72.1–7; 85.8–13
Philippians 4.6–9; 1 Timothy 2.1–6; James 3.13–18
Matthew 5.43–end; John 14.23–29; *or* 15.9–17

Social Justice and Responsibility

Isaiah 32.15–end; Amos 5.21–24; *or* 8.4–7; Acts 5.1–11
Psalms 31.21–24; 85.1–7; 146.5–10
Colossians 3.12–15; James 2.1–4
Matthew 5.1–12; *or* 25.31–end; Luke 16.19–end

Ministry, including Ember Days

(See page 7)

Numbers 11.16–17, 24–29; *or* 27.15–end; 1 Samuel 16.1–13*a*; Isaiah 6.1–8; *or* 61.1–3; Jeremiah 1.4–10
Psalms 40.8–13; 84.8–12; 89.19–25; 101.1–5, 7; 122
Acts 20.28–35; 1 Corinthians 3.3–11; Ephesians 4.4–16; Philippians 3.7–14
Luke 4.16–21; *or* 12.35–43; *or* 22.24–27; John 4.31–38; *or* 15.5–17

In Time of Trouble

Genesis 9.8–17; Job 1.13–end; Isaiah 38.6–11
Psalms 86.1–7; 107.4–15; 142.1–7
Romans 3.21–26; Romans 8.18–25; 2 Corinthians 8.1–5, 9
Mark 4.35–end; Luke 12.1–7; John 16.31–end

For the Sovereign

Joshua 1.1–9; Proverbs 8.1–16
Psalms 20; 101; 121
Romans 13.1–10; Revelation 21.22—22.4
Matthew 22.16–22; Luke 22.24–30

The anniversary of HM The King's accession is 8 September.

¶ *Psalms in the Course of a Month*

The following provision may be used for a monthly cycle of psalmody in place of the psalms provided in the tables in this booklet. It is based on the provision in The Book of Common Prayer.

	Morning Prayer	**Evening Prayer**
1	1—5	6—8
2	9—11	12—14
3	15—17	18
4	19—21	22—23
5	24—26	27—29
6	30—31	32—34
7	35—36	37
8	38—40	41—43
9	44—46	47—49
10	50—52	53—55
11	56—58	59—61
12	62—64	65—67
13	68	69—70
14	71—72	73—74
15	75—77	78
16	79—81	82—85
17	86—88	89
18	90—92	93—94
19	95—97	98—101
20	102—103	104
21	105	106
22	107	108—109
23	110—112	113—115
24	116—118	119.1–32
25	119.33–72	119.73–96
26	119.97–144	119.145–176
27	120—125	126—131
28	132—135	136—138
29	139—140	141—143
30	144—146	147—150

In February the psalms are read only to the 28th or 29th day of the month.

In January, March, May, July, August, October and December, all of which have 31 days, the same psalms are read on the last day of the month (being an ordinary weekday) which were read the day before, or else the psalms of the monthly course omitted on one of the Sundays in that month.

Concise Calendar November 2025 – December 2026

Advent 2025 to the eve of Advent 2026: Year A (Daily Eucharistic Lectionary Year 2)

November 2025						
Sunday		4bAdv	3bAdv	2bAdv	ChrK	Adv1
Monday		3	10	17	24	
Tuesday		4	11	18	25	
Wednesday		5	12	19	26	
Thursday		6	13	20	27	
Friday		7	14	21	28	
Saturday	**AllSs**	8	15	22	29	

December 2025					
Sunday		Adv2	Adv3	Adv4	Chr1
Monday	1	8	15	22	29
Tuesday	2	9	16	23	30
Wednesday	3	10	17	24	31
Thursday	4	11	18	**Chr**	
Friday	5	12	19	26	
Saturday	6	13	20	27	

January 2026					
Sunday		Chr2	Bapt	Ep2	Ep3
Monday		5	12	19	26
Tuesday		**Epiph**	13	20	27
Wednesday		7	14	21	28
Thursday	1	8	15	22	29
Friday	2	9	16	23	30
Saturday	3	10	17	24	31

February 2026					
Sunday		Ep4	2bLnt	NbLnt	Lnt1
Monday		**Pres**	9	16	23
Tuesday		3	10	17	24
Wednesday		4	11	**AshW**	25
Thursday		5	12	19	26
Friday		6	13	20	27
Saturday		7	14	21	28

March 2026					
Sunday	Lnt2	Lnt3	Lnt4	Lnt5	**PmS**
Monday	2	9	16	23	30
Tuesday	3	10	17	24	31
Wednesday	4	11	18	**Ann**	
Thursday	5	12	19	26	
Friday	6	13	20	27	
Saturday	7	14	21	28	

April 2026					
Sunday		**Est**	Est2	Est3	Est4
Monday		6	13	20	27
Tuesday		7	14	21	28
Wednesday	1	8	15	22	29
Thursday	**MTh**	9	16	23	30
Friday	**GFr**	10	17	24	
Saturday	4	11	18	25	

May 2026						
Sunday		Est5	Est6	Est7	**Pent**	**TrS**
Monday		4	11	18	25	
Tuesday		5	12	19	26	
Wednesday		6	13	20	27	
Thursday		7	**Ascn**	21	28	
Friday	1	8	15	22	29	
Saturday	2	9	16	23	30	

June 2026					
Sunday		Tr1	Tr2	Tr3	Tr4
Monday	1	8	15	22	29
Tuesday	2	9	16	23	30
Wednesday	3	10	17	24	
Thursday	4	11	18	25	
Friday	5	12	19	26	
Saturday	6	13	20	27	

July 2026					
Sunday		Tr5	Tr6	Tr7	Tr8
Monday		6	13	20	27
Tuesday		7	14	21	28
Wednesday	1	8	15	22	29
Thursday	2	9	16	23	30
Friday	3	10	17	24	31
Saturday	4	11	18	25	

August 2026						
Sunday		Tr9	Tr10	Tr11	Tr12	Tr13
Monday		3	10	17	24	31
Tuesday		4	11	18	25	
Wednesday		5	12	19	26	
Thursday		6	13	20	27	
Friday		7	14	21	28	
Saturday	1	8	15	22	29	

September 2026					
Sunday		Tr14	Tr15	Tr16	Tr17
Monday		7	14	21	28
Tuesday	1	8	15	22	29
Wednesday	2	9	16	23	30
Thursday	3	10	17	24	
Friday	4	11	18	25	
Saturday	5	12	19	26	

October 2026					
Sunday		Tr18	Tr19	Tr20	LstTr
Monday		5	12	19	26
Tuesday		6	13	20	27
Wednesday		7	14	21	28
Thursday	1	8	15	22	29
Friday	2	9	16	23	30
Saturday	3	10	17	24	31

November 2026					
Sunday	**AllSs**	3bAdv	2bAdv	ChrK	Adv1
Monday	2	9	16	23	30
Tuesday	3	10	17	24	
Wednesday	4	11	18	25	
Thursday	5	12	19	26	
Friday	6	13	20	27	
Saturday	7	14	21	28	

December 2026					
Sunday		Adv2	Adv3	Adv4	Chr1
Monday		7	14	21	28
Tuesday	1	8	15	22	29
Wednesday	2	9	16	23	30
Thursday	3	10	17	24	31
Friday	4	11	18	**Chr**	
Saturday	5	12	19	26	

On Sunday 28 December 2025 The Holy Innocents may be celebrated.

On Sunday 4 January **The Epiphany** may be celebrated, transferred from 6 January.

On Sunday 25 January The Conversion of Paul may be celebrated.

On Sunday 1 February **The Presentation** may be celebrated, transferred from 2 February.

On Sunday 18 October Luke the Evangelist may be celebrated.

On Sunday 27 December 2026 John, Apostle and Evangelist may be celebrated.